Modern L   ning
Strategies

Every secondary school pupil studies Modern Foreign Languages as part of the curriculum. Research into language teaching and learning suggests that certain individuals have unconsciously developed a wide range of tactics or strategies to make their learning effective – they are 'good' language learners. Much of the research so far has focused on adult learners of English. This book extends the research to secondary school pupils learning French, German or Spanish and discusses the principles underlying Learning Strategies. Practical examples are also provided of how strategies can be taught to help teachers get the best results from their pupils. It is divided into two sections.

The first section sets out Learning Strategies as part of a theoretical understanding of how languages are learned. It traces curriculum reform in Modern Foreign Languages in recent times and the rise of the Communicative Approach. It argues that learners need to learn 'how to learn' if they are to use language independently. The strategies of a group of learners at different points in their learning are explored as a way of showing what strategies look like in practice.

The second section gives guidelines for classroom activities involving Learning Strategies and shows how Strategy Instruction may be undertaken by teachers in order to help learners make use of them. Details are included of the work of five case study teachers employing such instruction in their classrooms.

The book concludes with reflections on the current political and educational climate, arguing for the need to link theory and practice, both in educational research and teachers' continuing professional development.

Michael Grenfell is Senior Lecturer in Educational Studies at the Centre for Language in Education at the University of Southampton. **Vee Harris** is Lecturer in Modern Languages in Education at Goldsmiths College, University of London.

Modern Languages and Learning Strategies

In theory and practice

**Michael Grenfell
and Vee Harris**

Routledge
Taylor & Francis Group

LONDON AND NEW YORK

First published 1999
by Routledge
11 New Fetter Lane, London EC4P 4EE

Simultaneously published in the USA and Canada
by Routledge
29 West 35th Street, New York, NY 10001

Routledge is an imprint of the Taylor & Francis Group

Transferred to Digital Printing 2003

Typeset in Goudy by
Keystroke, Jacaranda Lodge, Wolverhampton
Printed and bound in Great Britain by
Selwood Printing Ltd, West Sussex

British Library Cataloguing in Publication Data
A catalogue record for this book is available from the British Library

Library of Congress Cataloging in Publication Data
Grenfell, Michael, 1953–
    Learning modern languages : modern languages and learning
strategies in teaching and practice / Michael Grenfell and Vee
Harris.
      p.   cm.
    Includes bibliographical references and index.
    1. Languages, Modern—Study and teaching. I. Harris, Vee, 1949– .
II. Title.
    PB35.G783   1999
    418′.0071′2—dc21
                                              98–54121
                                              CIP

ISBN 0–415–21340–1 (hbk)
ISBN 0–415–17868–1 (pbk)

For Cherry, Matthew and Sophie

Contents

Figures

Tables

Acknowledgements

We would like to acknowledge the professional initiative and commitment of Angelina Adams, Marion Carty, Pamela Dewey, Jacqui Footman and Fiona Lunskey. Many of the ideas presented in Part Two of this book stem from our work with them and their subsequent experiences in applying the ideas presented in Part One in their classrooms.

We also acknowledge the students on our respective teacher-training and postgraduate courses at the University of Southampton and Goldsmiths College (in particular, Linsey Hand) for their enthusiasm and imagination in also working with the idea of 'learning to learn'.

We would also like to thank our case-study learners for making time available to us, and undertaking the tasks we gave them with patience and a willingness to help us in our investigations.

We are grateful to Ann Swarbrick (the Open University) who first showed us the Dutch poem.

Cheryl Hardy read the manuscript and made numerous helpful suggestions and comments.

Rita Corbidge showed work and commitment beyond the call of duty in creating a tidy manuscript.

Without all these, the book would not have been possible.

We would also like to thank CILT for permission to reproduce extracts from Harris, V. (1997) *Teaching Learners How to Learn*, and HMSO for permission to reproduce extracts from *Modern Foreign Languages in the National Curriculum*.

Introduction

Why a book on learner strategies?

Modern languages teaching over the past decade or so has moved from more or less traditional approaches, involving the explicit teaching of grammar and translation, to various versions of communicative methodology. In England, the communicative accent has been reflected in the Graded Objectives movement, the General Certificate of Secondary Education (GCSE) and the reform of Advanced Level syllabuses. However, despite this trend and the appearance of a plethora of attractive and authentic language-teaching materials, there has been a growing concern that learners have not progressed as much as might have been anticipated. Furthermore, learners are not developing independent language use; in short, they lack linguistic autonomy.

In parallel to these methodological developments, applied linguistic research has continued to investigate the processes of second-language acquisition. The search has been to discover what is inside the 'black box' of the human brain so that teaching methods might be designed to facilitate rather than hinder the learning process. Part of this research has focused on the 'good language learner' and what strategies they adopt to be successful.

This book sets out to investigate these issues and topics. Much of the research literature on second-language acquisition and strategies deals with the learning of English by adults. A great deal has been discovered about the learning process. This book takes these findings as a starting point and develops the discussion in the context of modern languages (French, German, Spanish) teaching and learning within the English secondary school age range (11–18 years). Our intent is to set out the theoretical principles and practical justifications for studying learning strategies and working to develop them with our learners. Underpinning this discussion is a desire to enhance classroom methodology and promote autonomous language learners. Raising achievement is a central concern of every modern-languages teacher these days. We believe that improved learning comes through improved teaching, which in turn is the result of better methodological understanding on the part of teachers. A central aim of this book is to develop such understanding but to do so within the practical constraints of nationally prescribed curricula: in the case of the British context, the National Curriculum; GCSE; National Vocational Qualifications (NVQs).

The book is divided into two parts: the first deals with what strategies are and what they might look like in practice; the second part concerns practical ideas for developing strategies with learners. The second part also looks at what happened when one group of teachers set about teaching their pupils 'how to learn'.

Chapter 1 sets out the context for our concern with learning strategies. A brief history of the past two decades of methodological reform is given as well as some historical perspectives to show what brought us to our present understanding of how modern languages should be taught and learned. We show how this search for methodology has run in parallel and sometimes given rise to the development of approaches for second-language teaching and learning. The English example is used as a case in point of syllabus reform which seeks to improve linguistic development. The 'communicative movement' gets special attention, and the ways this has been specifically interpreted for modern-languages teaching. We also look at the issue of methodological disappointments and what the issues and concerns have been when outcome has not matched objectives.

Chapter 2 deals with the research literature on second-language acquisition. It begins with a consideration of the ways researchers have attempted to conceptualise language and its underlying processes. The whole issue of a model for learning is addressed. We then consider the literature on the 'good language learner' and look at what these students do. The notion of 'strategy' is introduced, and what various strategies look like in practice. This discussion is connected with a specific learning model – that of cognitive theory – in order to show how a consideration of general learning strategies also tells us something about the processes of second-language learning. What research on learning strategies implies for the context we are addressing is also considered, as well as the issue of developing autonomy with learners.

Chapter 3 presents three case examples of learners at very different stages in their language learning; from the beginner to advanced student. We see how they each approached their language learning, what their strengths and weaknesses are, and how they differed from each other. We also suggest what other strategies they each might use in order to maximise their learning. Various other issues and questions about strategy use are addressed; namely, what are their cognitive characters and how developmental sequencing might vary according to the stage learners have reached.

Chapter 4 is the first of the mainly practical chapters. Here, the whole issue of 'strategy instruction' is addressed. We refer to what others have done and how they have fared, before dealing systematically with sequences which might be followed in directing learners in their own strategy use. Examples for actual classroom use are provided, based on listening, speaking, reading and writing. Memorisation strategies are also included. Finally, we discuss some reservations which researchers have sometimes expressed in working with strategies with learners.

Chapter 5 covers teacher–practitioners' exploration of the effectiveness of strategy training or instruction. Accounts of these teachers using strategies are given which highlight a range of issues in their practical implementation. We look at individual pupils' responses in terms of their personality and learning styles. We also consider what these experiences tell us about how to organise strategy instruction in order to maximise its effectiveness.

Since a central concern of the book is the development of autonomy, the reader is invited to construct their own pathway through its varying sections according to their individual needs and interests. For some, Part Two might provide an appropriate starting point, embarking directly on Strategy Instruction, and then using Part One as an opportunity to reflect on their experiences in the context of the background research. Others may prefer to consider the rationale underlying Strategy Instruction before exploring how it can be implemented in the classroom.

In our Conclusion to the book we revisit questions of progression and autonomy as a measure of linguistic competence. We focus on the issue of balance in modern-languages teaching methodology: between theory and practice, research and literature, intention and reality. Our aim here is to underline the importance of learning strategies for both the learner and the teacher. We set this within an agenda of language teaching and teacher professional development for the advent of the new millennium. The notion of 'learning to learn' forms a coda to our discussion.

Part One

1 Modern-languages teaching: in search of methodology

In this chapter, we set out the background to modern-languages teaching and learning over the past few decades. We do so in order to provide a basis for answering such questions as: what are learning strategies? Why are they significant? It shows the conceptual roots to our present methodological approaches and explains the current preoccupation with learning strategies. This preoccupation entails shifts of emphasis over methodology in how the learner is viewed and in the pedagogical role of the teacher. Before considering learning strategies, the processes they involve and their practical significance in the classroom, it is necessary to know something about what has led to the present position in understanding how modern languages are taught and learned. The context for this book is modern-languages teaching and learning in Britain. However, despite a traditional reputation for sociocultural inward-lookingness, British modern linguists have never operated a 'closed-shop' policy when it comes to matters of pedagogy – quite the contrary. The tale of this chapter is therefore often one of progressive inventiveness and high methodological ambition. In the course of development and reform, teachers, researchers and policy makers have drawn upon a wide repertoire of theories and methods. This chapter shows how it has been so.

Decades of reform

This book is being published on the cusp of the new millennium. We are moving into a new era in all respects. As we move forward, it is natural not only to look to the future, but also to reflect back on the past. Our present century which is coming to a close is one that has been dominated by language. The revolution in communications can be summed up as a question of the directness and speed of human contact. Not so long ago the only way of communicating with someone not readily at hand was to write a message and send it overland. The journey could be perilous, and there was no guarantee that the message would be delivered. If it was, there could be problems of interpretation, clarification might be called for, and events may have already superseded what was being communicated. Where the written word was not an option, individuals resorted to visual signals, which could only convey the most basic messages. The invention of telecommunications put people at a distance in direct contact for the first time. The technology expanded fast. Telegrams were replaced by the telephone. Telephone contact became less a bookable event, surrounded by bureaucracy, than an immediate, personal option. All four corners of the world are now literally at the other end of a telephone line. Contact can be established independently simply by dialling the necessary code. And now, in the last decade of the twentieth century, as the presence of the Internet in our lives grows at a seemingly unstoppable pace, written documents can be exchanged on-line with countries on the other side of the globe. The Web is awash with printed information. Electronic mail puts individuals in direct contact in a way that means they do not even have to be in conversation with each other in order to exchange all manner of documentation, personal information and financial commitments.

Alongside these technological developments, the world of ideas has become most preoccupied with the form and substance of language. Increased participation and audiences in telecommunications have underlined the necessity to handle language. The field of philosophy, that most refined discipline of enquiry into human affairs, has focused increasingly on language; so much so that contemporary philosophy of human thought is really a philosophy of language. In all areas of the human and physical sciences, modernist ideals have given way to postmodernist doubts, founded, for the most part, on linguistic insecurity; that language does not always convey or represent what is intended. The power of language has increasingly been scrutinised, and found to act in ways which privilege and subvert (see, for example, Bourdieu 1991). The fabric of language itself has been taken apart and shown to be infinitely malleable (see, for example, Taylor 1992).

Briefly, then, it is against this sociolinguistic background that language teaching and learning have developed their own idiosyncratic course. How we teach and how we learn languages is often informed by the direct experience of teachers and learners. However, a new science of applied language studies has grown up in the past hundred years or so which specifically investigates language learning with the supposed intent of facilitating this process however it takes place. The founding father of contemporary linguistics, Ferdinand de Saussure, has also been adopted by postmodernists and philosophers, who use his theories on the nature and processes of language. Saussure's *Course in Applied Linguistics* was published in 1916 by his students as a collection of lecture notes after his death three years earlier, and immediately set the agenda for both pure and applied linguistics. Nearly a century later, we continue to work with and develop his basic founding principles. Contemporary linguistic theory and research has had much to say about what language is and how it is processed. By implication, many applied linguists have sought to establish the way languages are learned and the nature of competence in a language. From this work, it is a short step to attempting to recommend didactic methodology as a facilitator to language learning – and it is in this tradition that we situate ourselves in this book. Before addressing current pedagogical issues, however, we want to say a little more about the paths which have brought us to our present methodological concerns. First, it is important to realise that principles of language teaching were not born with contemporary linguistics but pre-date them.

In the early part of this century, the direct method was advocated as an effective means of teaching a foreign language. Here, 'the essential condition for acquiring a real command of a language . . . is to establish in connection with that language the same Direct Association between experience and expression as exists in the use of the mother-tongue' (Board of Education Circular 797 (1912) quoted in Hawkins 1987, p. 132). In these few words, the major issues of the pedagogic debate on second-language learning are set; namely, the similarities and differences between learning one's first language and another foreign language. The similarities and differences are of process and function, which are significant ultimately in terms of how they are understood and what is made of them in a formal teaching context. Briefly stated: is it sufficient to approach the learning and teaching of a second language as a replication of what is involved in learning a first language from birth? The Direct Method seems to reply in the affirmative to this question. Later on in this chapter there is discussion of the controversy surrounding a more recent methodological debate along similar lines – that of the so-called 'communicative' movement and the work of Stephen Krashen. However, even in the early part of the century, this assertion was challenged. In a much quoted statement, Harold Palmer wrote on the tensions in linking what we think we know about languages with how we subsequently believe they should be taught. 'Ce n'est pas la méthode qui nous manque', he asserted 'c'est la base même de la méthode' (1917). In other words, we do not lack formal descriptions of ways to teach, they are numerous. What is harder to establish is a sound basis for methodology, as clearly, no one has yet discovered *the* method.

The picture of methodological ambition and disappointment is graphically illustrated by Eric Hawkins in his review of modern languages in the curriculum (1987). Here, he lists over forty 'names of the game' (p. 306). It is worth pausing to name some of them:

The New Method	The Analytical Method
The Newer Method	The Concrete Method
The Reform Method	The Conversational Method
The Natural Method	The Anti-classical Method
The Rational Method	The Anti-grammatical Method
The Correct Method	The Anti-translational Method
The Sensible Method	The Psychological Method
The Direct Method	The Reading Method
The Phonetical Method	The Drip-feed Method
The Phonetical Transcription Method	The Active Method
	The Eclectic Method
The Imitative Method	The Dual Language Method

Of course, in their chosen titles, many of them reveal the approach they take: and there are many, many more. Each has had its advocates. Some have had their disciples. All of them have had their relative degrees of success and failure. But, none have proved that they can work all the time, in all cases. There are simply too many variables: age, culture, context, personal preferences, external support, individual learning differences, and so on. What works in one time and place does not necessarily work elsewhere. However, within the disappointments which each method has necessarily experienced, it is probably worth reminding ourselves that people have indeed learned languages. They always have and they always will. Methodology alone can never be a solution to language learning. Rather, it is an aid and a support. This might lead us to ask: if effective language learning does not depend on a particular methodology, what does it depend on? It is in response to questions like these that this book has been written; why and how students learn languages has been our *raison d'être*. But, for the moment, it is worth pausing to consider more fully the relation between learning process and didactic methodology.

Shaping language learning: a national example

Methodology is a problematic issue. Although all the terms listed above are followed by the word 'method', there are vastly different practices included within each title: some proceeding through a highly prescribed set of sequences, others more loosely based around general principles. Such a distinction was realised by Anthony in the early 1960s when he wrote about the differences between *approach, method* and *technique* (1963). For him, a method is indeed an explicit plan for the presentation of materials to learners. It often follows a pre-set series or set of stages, each with a particular functional role in the overall didactic design. Approach, on the other hand, is more straightforwardly axiomatic, and follows the principles underlying the form of teaching taken. Finally, technique refers to the actual classroom activities used in implementing the approach or method. Such techniques presumably attempt to put principles into practice in terms of what they require the learner to do and what underlying justification there is for this. Anthony implied some sort of hierarchy in the relationship between these three. In other words, approach was superordinate to method; in fact, might include several methods. Technique was the practical manifestation of these methods and was consistent with them and the general approach to which they were related. Implicit in such a hierarchy is again the problematic relation between actual didactic activity and what we think we know and understand about the nature of language and the processes of acquiring it. The turbulence of this relation has become more acutely felt in recent years as methodological disappointments have set in. So much is this the case, that 'method' has become a term about which we are suspicious, and it has become more common to consider 'approach' the more helpful title when dealing with what goes on in the classroom. Approach has the advantage of being less prescriptive and even allowing techniques which might on the surface at least appear to be contradictory; for example the use of both target language and the mother tongue as part of classroom discourse.

Such issues and arguments concerning the nature of methodology can be seen in the history of modern-languages teaching in Britain in recent decades. This history might best be understood as a move from *method* – in this case, the grammar–translation and various audio-visual/audio-lingual methods – to the increasing adoption of a general *approach* to planning for language learning and teaching in pedagogic contexts. It is worth taking time to reconsider these in a little more detail.

Grammar–translation method

The most dominant second-language teaching methodology of recent time is probably the grammar–translation method. Its origins can be traced back to the annals of history, where the only languages considered worth learning were Latin and Greek. The way to learn them amounted to little more than analysis of grammar and memorisation of rules and vocabulary through classical texts. Even when Greek and Latin were joined by French and German in the nineteenth century as precursors to modern foreign-languages learning, teaching consisted primarily of organising grammar items for analysis and application. Reading and writing predominated, and oral skills were seen as very much secondary aims. The purpose of this study was to increase an individual's culture and wit, and extend the discipline of the mind in abstract matters. Grammar rules were taught deductively and used for textual analysis and comparisons. The accuracy of resulting translations into and from English were a mark of proficiency and competence in mastering a language. English therefore dominated in the foreign-languages classroom, as did literary expression. Accuracy was all.

These characteristics conjure up a foreboding picture of the foreign-languages classroom on which a thousand stereotypical images have been built. It shows the worst excesses of tedious analysis and unusable knowledge of a language. Classes were dull for all but the classically inclined; their practical usefulness almost non-existent. And yet as a method, it continued well into the post second-war period, and, it could be argued, has continued to provide the bedrock of most methods to this day; including those seemingly diametrically opposed at first sight to its basic tenets; for example, audio-lingualism. As outmoded as the grammar–translation method might now seem, its very form and expression does raise a number of significant issues, which continue to be pertinent to modern-languages teaching and learning to this day. Indeed, such issues have yet to be fully addressed in a satisfactory way, and this book is one latest contribution to the continuing pedagogical debate. It is worth listing some of the most important questions now in an informal manner as a way of anticipating their significance in later discussion in the following chapters.

What does it mean to 'know' a second language?
What is the relationship between an individual's first and second language?
Are first and second-language-learning processes the same?
What is 'grammar'?

What is a grammar rule?
What is the relationship between the formal grammar of a textbook and the
psychological grammar held in the mind in order to generate language?
What is the connection between written and spoken language?
What is the role of formal instruction in acquiring linguistic competence?
Can formally expressed rules be taught, learned, and applied in practice?
How does one individual differ from another?
How important is the topic content of language used in foreign-language
lessons?
What is the role of linguistic context?

Clearly, many of these questions are only present in their absence in
the grammar–translation method, or implied by the practice adopted. What
is ignored by a method is as important to the practice it generates as what is
explicitly prescribed by the method. The fundamental question remains,
however: how does didactic method relate to internal linguistic process?

As can be seen from this discussion of the grammar–translation method,
the stimulation for acquisition and conceptualisation of how to learn a second
foreign language came from a classical view of education, not necessarily from the
ideas to be found in linguistics about the way languages were learned. However,
by the 1930s a new understanding of language appeared. It appeared as part of a
new paradigm in the human sciences: behaviourism.

Behaviourism

Behaviourism is probably now and forever associated with the image of rote
obedience to learned practices; for example, with rats getting their food supply by
setting off the operation of a sequence of mechanisms. In essence, this approach
to psychology is based on stimulus and response. Its linguistic form appeared
in the 1930s in structural linguistics: the science of analysing language in terms of
its component parts. Structural linguists were not interested in what happens in
the human mind as such, but in the stimulus/response mechanisms observable as
the product of language. Language was just another form of human behaviour.
As such it was learned through exposure to 'correct' forms, response, and by
subsequent reinforcement.

This approach to language and language learning spawned one of the most
influential styles of teaching; namely, audio-visual and audio-lingual methods.
These methods were at their height in the 1960s: no language class was complete
without a set of slides and accompanying tapes, and expensive language laboratories were installed. Classes would consist of exposure to stock phrases, which
were repeated by the learner until learned by heart. Questions and answers proceeded in a similar way. If the learner made mistakes, it was because insufficient
practice had been undertaken. Such errors could therefore be eliminated by
further practice. Repetition drills were the order of the day. Phonological and
syntactical forms were selected for their structural significance. Language

students learned these through induction rather than explicit analysis. Increased competence was defined in terms of gaining a larger repertoire of structures and forms, which could then be applied in real-life contexts. Good language learners gained good linguistic habits through drilling and practice.

Clearly, these techniques were very different from those so central to the grammar–translation method. Besides a diametrically opposed view of how to 'learn' grammar, audio-lingual methods stressed oral–aural work in a way hitherto unknown to teachers used to traditional analytical approaches. Visual associations were often central to the learning process; as in the audio-visual offspring to audio-lingualism.

The time-lag between the development of these theories of language and learning and the prominence of their practical application is, of course, an issue. Structural linguistics and language behaviourism were at their academic height in the 1930s and were fundamentally superseded by the 1960s. However, in pedagogic circles, in Britain at least, it was precisely during the 1960s that this style of language teaching, audio-lingual and audio-visual, took hold in schools. Tapes and film strips were *de rigueur* for modern-languages departments and the market was flooded by a vast array of courses aimed precisely at supplying the learner with opportunities to repeat, repeat and repeat. Repetition of stock phrases, and the drilling of stock question–answer forms were all.

Interestingly, many of these courses were used without entirely abandoning the grammar–translation method, and it was not unusual to find the two running along together side by side in unhappy union. In these cases, explicit grammar analysis took place prior to or following exposure to it through audio-lingual drilling. Reinforcement also might take in grammatical applications through such activities as translation and dictation.

As in the case of the grammar–translation method, behaviourism lives on today in a range of audio-lingual courses. And language laboratories are still common. One other significant influence of the audio-linguistic fashion is the focus it gave to linguistic context. Much of the material was based around people, imaginary or real, dealing with realistic social situations. An underlying assumption in this approach was that languages were being learned to be used. This belief found resonance with the widening horizons brought about by the technological boom of the 1960s, together with the greater opportunity to travel and the opening of international markets.

The audio-lingual method was, however, flawed. Pupils found the drilling unengaging, and progress was consequently slow. Grammar was as difficult as ever. The inductive transfer seldom seemed to take place. Most damning of all, many of the stock phrases simply did not work in real life. Even before the audio-linguistic revolution in foreign-languages teaching in British schools in the 1960s, Chomskyan linguistics had fatally wounded the behaviourist assumptions on which it was based. But it was to be many more years before such academic changes in understanding were to have any influence in the classroom. In Britain, the hybrid methodology of grammar–translation and audio-lingualism was further developed in the 1970s and early 1980s in a form of situational language teaching, or the 'new' direct method. Here, elements from both were taken and deliberately mixed: visual presentation; isolation and drilling of structural grammar; repetition of question–answer sequences; oral–aural emphasis; contextualised language. Grammar was dealt with both inductively and deductively. For example, initial presentation was orally based and not explicitly defined. However, subsequently, the grammar rule was made explicit and then reinforced with grammar exercises in which the main points were tested. Progress linguistically was defined in terms of mastery of a number of grammatical structures and the level of the sophistication and accuracy displayed in their application. Complexity was all. But another revolution was just around the corner: communicative language teaching.

The road to communicative language teaching

One interesting feature of this brief account of a history of foreign-languages teaching in this country is the relationship between different fields of ideas: academic study of linguistics and practical methodologies; practice in modern-languages teaching and learning and the teaching of English as a foreign language (EFL). The latter is worth some consideration. It is a well-known fact that English has developed as a lingua franca and is extensively taught at an international level. This has been reinforced by e-mail and Internet, where English is often used as the base language. Modern languages, on the other hand, are much more parochial, and, traditionally have only been taught to the most able, rather as a mark of academic distinction than as an aid to work and travel as in the case of English. The upshot of this situation is that English-language teaching and learning has always been the more robust of the two areas of study; the one which has attracted most resources; the most frequent object of research and enquiry into its processes; the language in which methodological innovation first appeared. The methodological response to changes in the world of linguistics has therefore impacted with less time delay in English as a foreign language than in modern languages. The change from audio-lingualism and situational language teaching to communicative language teaching in EFL came about more directly as a result of new discoveries in the nature and process of language than the same move in modern languages. Certainly, by the late 1960s, when the hybrid course of grammar–translation and audio-visual methods was at its zenith in British secondary schools, those involved in EFL realised that the model of language on which these methods were based had been superseded. Behaviourism and structural linguistics had simply had their day. The source of this theoretical undermining was Noam Chomsky and Chomskyan linguistics which he initiated.

Chomskyan linguistics

In key works (1957, 1965) Chomsky's attack on behaviourism and structural linguistics was full-frontal and definitive. His main defining argument was that language could not be a habit-forming exercise of stimulus, response and reinforcement since language is generated anew in each new utterance. There were not a finite number of structures which had to be learned and applied. Rather an infinite number of linguistic forms were generated from a fixed set of principles and parameters. This realisation led him to argue for the existence of a *universal grammar*, which was a product of the biological structure of the human brain. As its name suggests, this grammar is common to all human beings. It follows that all languages share it, but this commonality is at a deep level since we clearly do not understand all human languages and the grammatical systems of various languages are obviously very different. There is then a distinction between *deep syntactic structures*, which share the universal grammar and *surface structures* which differ from one language to another.

In Chomskyian linguistics learning a first language amounts to developing competence in that language. However, this is not a process of structural accumulation but mind-setting in which the various grammatical options for that language are established. A simple example may illustrate this point.

We know that the position of the adverb differs between English and French:

He *often* eats at home	Il dîne *souvent* chez lui
We *never* go out	Nous ne sortons *jamais*
I *only* have two pounds	Je n'ai *que* deux livres

Chomsky argues that in one's first language each of these are not learned discretely as a structural possibility. Rather, the whole positioning is set in linguistic development; not only for one adverb, but all others. Clearly, it does matter whether a baby is brought up to be French or English. However, biologically either form is possible, and it is only through exposure that the appropriate form is set at a deep psycholinguistic level. It is in this way that any one individual's so-called 'competence' in a language is established. Competence here might be defined as the formation of all possible generating structures in the mind, of which any one structural element is a product. The common name for the latter is 'performance'.

Chomsky was the first to assert that he did not know what this discovery implied for the learning of a second language, still less for a teaching methodology. However, the effect on the way we view language, its nature and processes was total; so much so that all linguistic and learning theory now defines itself in terms of its relation (near or far) to Chomskyan linguistics. The most commonly shared concept in linguistics and language learning is that of *competence*: that knowing languages is really a matter of the degree to which a psychological mind-set has been established for any one individual. As such, it is particular to them, shares something of their own life trajectory and identity, and is a product of their own individual learning development. From this position, it is easy to see how everything follows on from the idea that the aim in teaching and learning a second language must be to develop competence in that language, and this must entail establishing generating structures at a deep psychological level.

Chomskyian linguistics has evolved into a highly technical form of analysis and expression involving the study of transformation grammar in synchronic moments. What it has little room for is language in its social environment, and it is this dimension to which early writers on communicative language teaching turned. In a way, it might be said that they took Chomskyian linguistics, if only in the form of its attack on existing models of learning, and socialised it. Developing competence in a language then became developing the ability to communicate; now referred to as 'communicative competence'.

Chomsky, in his efforts to make linguistics a precise science, infamously claimed that its primary concerns were the *ideal speaker–listener*, the *homogeneous speech community*, and *perfect language knowledge*. In this view of the speaker–listener, limitations of memory, distractions, shifts of attention are an irrelevance (see Chomsky, 1965). In other words, Chomskyian linguistics is concerned with the *ideal* competence of a language rather than individual performance events. As such, many have observed that it addresses something that never exists in real-time. But the notion of competence has persisted.

Del Hymes, the linguistic anthropologist, was the first to use the term 'communicative competence' to contrast with Chomsky's ideal competence. Hymes's celebrated statement that 'there are rules of use without which the rules of grammar would be useless' (1972) perfectly captures his attack on Chomskyian idealism and his attempt to contrast it with his own 'socialised' view of language. For Hymes, it is not only if something is grammatically possible in a language that matters, but whether it is *feasible* and *appropriate*. This notion introduces a whole lot of social values and conventions which are *rule* governed; in other words, they follow specific practices. The major conclusion from this view is that learning a language involves not only mastering grammatical accuracy, developing syntactic competence, but also acquiring the paralinguistic and metalinguistic features involved in performing a linguistic act in an acceptable manner.

Once this understanding of competence in a language is taken on board, then it is clear that previous methodologies are found to be sadly lacking. Grammar-translation simply underplays the importance of interaction in the language, and the social practices this involves. The same might be said for audio-lingualism, which also fails to teach language in a way which is sensitive to the shifting repertoire of its realisation. The notion of communicative competence tries to include all these dimensions: the grammatical and the social.

Since its inception into academic and pedagogic debate, communicative competence has become an established concept for formally expressing the general aims and objectives of language learning and teaching. Figure 1.1 illustrates three of its major versions; and also demonstrates the way in which a particular element in the discussion on language learning has developed over time.

Canale and Swain (1980) and Canale (1983) set out four specific features of communicative competence: grammatical competence; sociolinguistic competence; discourse competence and strategic competence. Grammatical competence indicates knowledge of the necessary syntactic rules in a language – what is

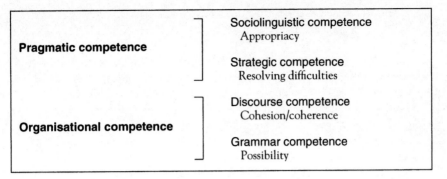

Figure 1.1 Conceptualising communicative competence
Sources: Bachman 1990; Hymes 1972; Canale and Swain 1980; Canale 1983.

possible in a formal Chomskyian sense. Sociolinguistic competence refers to knowledge of the changing social situations in which language occurs, as well as the roles necessary for effective exchanges. Discourse competence concerns the way particular speech and written elements of language form part of a larger discourse or text, and so must be connected operationally. Finally, strategic competence entails the range of practices individuals use in order to exert some control over communication: how to hold conversations and repair breakdowns in communication.

Bachman (1990) is a more recent attempt to develop the notion of communicative competence. Here, competence in a language is broken down into its formal, organisational features such as structural elements (morphology, vocabulary, syntax, cohesion, etc.) and its practical or pragmatic operations (the substantive end to which language is put as well as its natural variety in local site contexts). Bachman's model takes forward the subdivision of communicative competence presented by Canale and Swain. The underlying principle is the same, however: that gaining linguistic competence involves control over the mechanics of the language *and* the social and psychological functions to which it can be put to use.

Of course, this move from focusing on language *per se* to its social expression parallels moves since the 1960s from a positivist, quasi-physical view of research in the social sciences to a more qualitative, ethnographic concern to investigate real-life contexts. For example, until the 1960s, psychological research was semi-experimental and based largely on statistical analysis. Educational research viewed the formation of educational theory much in the same way as a physicist viewed scientific theory. Behaviourism and structural linguistics also adopted this approach. However, from the 1960s onwards, this perspective has been largely eclipsed by an increasing preoccupation with various social scientific disciplines in studying real-life processes (see Carr and Kemmis 1986, Grenfell 1998a). It is possible to see the social theoretical bases for communicative competence and communicative language teaching in theoretical terms other than straight linguistic. Besides the evolving preoccupation of linguistic discussion, Brumfit (1988) lists five other major theoretical sources for communicative language teaching: first, anthropology with its concern for social contexts and the 'speech events' taking place in them (Hymes [1967] 1972); second, sociolinguistics with its observation of the patterns of adjustment individuals make in changing from one situation to another and its demonstration that linguistic rules should be understood as probabilities rather than absolute ones (Labov 1972); third, social psychology for its mapping of affective judgements made between in- and out-groups and the way individuals converge or diverge from linguistic forms and the motivation they have for doing so (Giles 1977, Bourrhis 1982, Tajfel 1982); fourth, the concern in philosophy for speech acts (Austin 1962, Searle 1969), intentions and interpretations, and the notion of the 'co-operative principle' (Grice 1975) in linguistic interactions; finally, ethnomethodology, which add-resses the rules governing micro-interactions, the conventions followed in social activity (Garfinkel 1968). Each of these is concerned with a particular perspec-tive on the 'social', and language is central to all of them. Brumfit (1988, p. 7), sums up their commonalties. Language is:

(a) context-dependent;
(b) unstable within conventionally-determined limits;
(c) negotiable at all level of analysis, but particularly in meaning of particular terms;
(d) closely related to individuals' self-concept and identity.

We have taken some time to create a picture of the academic climate which surrounded the advent of communicative language teaching. It is one which stressed the social over the psychological, in which the linguistic ideas of Chomsky were influential, but often in an indirect manner, as something to react against rather than take inspiration from. Indeed, when communicative language teaching arrived in the 1970s, and quickly became influential in the teaching of English as a foreign language, it was almost entirely bereft of a formal learning theory of language. Psychology, it seemed, had little to say about the social reality of language and therefore offered nothing for didactic methods. It was from the social sciences and a broad view of human discourse that the early advocates of communicative language teaching (CLT) took their inspiration. However, there was one exception – the work of the psycholinguist Stephen Krashen – and before looking at the principles of CLT in detail we would like to consider his main arguments.

In many ways, Krashen places himself in a similar position to the social scientists mentioned above. His remarks are based on strong personal conviction formed from experience and observation in life. He believes he has seen what he describes. And yet he is also a psychologist. His work, and that of his associates, is often highly empirical, is based on semi-experimental research and includes sophisticated statistical analysis. From Chomsky, he takes the idea that, basically, language competence is a biological reality, a condition of the human mind. However, he extrapolates this idea from first to second-language learning. There is then, in his model, a *language acquisition device* (LAD) which only has to be activated for language learning to take place. The means to this activation is 'comprehensible input'; in other words, lots of exposure in the language being learned at a 'comprehensible level'. In fact, best learning takes place when the level is one step ahead of the learner, as this makes understanding likely, but leaves linguistic space into which the learner may move. For him, explicit grammar learning is but an adjunct and plays very little part in building up competence. Language is *acquired*, not learned. Grammar can operate to *monitor* accuracy, though the conditions for effective use of this are so constrained that it is likely to be a hindrance rather than an aid to learning. In this model, learning a second language is very much like learning a first language. It follows that it helps if the learner is not affectively inhibited; much as a baby learns without self-consciousness. Furthermore, language is acquired through a *natural* order which is common to all. In other words, a sequence is identifiable in the stages through which learners pass when gaining competence, and Krashen and his associates have spent a good deal of time and energy demonstrating this order in experimental conditions (see Krashen 1981, 1982).

It would be wrong to associate Krashen too closely with the early stages of communicative language teaching. He is American, while the early writers on CLT were mainly British. They were also coming from a background of pedagogic involvement, while Krashen was an academic linguist. Moreover, many writers on CLT were explicitly critical of what Krashen was arguing (see Brumfit 1984). However, there are three main points to connect him with CLT: first, his most influential work and writing was being produced at around the same time as the early books and papers on CLT appeared; second, he was probably the best-known linguist of his day; third, and perhaps unusually, he was an applied linguist who apparently had something quite specific to say about teaching. Mindful of Krashen's fate at the hands of linguistic researchers (e.g. McLaughlin 1978), few applied linguists since him have been tempted to draw pedagogic conclusions and make didactic recommendations on the basis of their research. Still, despite these criticisms, it is clear that there is enough which is common in spirit between CLT and Krashen's theories to resonate with all but those who undertake a more detailed, rigorous comparison of the two. The first and most important of these resonances is that the processes of learning a first and a second language are very similar. The second is that learning takes place through meaning-focused language. The third is that interactions with other people rather than the language itself is central to the learning process. The fourth is that the identity of the learner is central in the learning process, as are the conditions of the context in which they find themselves. This section has considered the linguistic background to recent trends in language-teaching methodology. CLT has been mentioned a great deal. It is time to consider its principles in detail.

Communicative language teaching in practice

Earlier in this chapter, we wrote about the distinction between approach, method and technique. Which is CLT? Of course, in one sense it can be claimed to be all three. There are certainly communicative *techniques*, and, in the early days at least, when CLT was associated with later versions of situational language teaching, it took on many aspects of a prescribed *method*. Nowadays, however, it is no longer common to talk about the communicative *method*. Rather, it has evolved into a general *approach*. Howatt (1984) writes about a weak and a strong version of CLT: the former referring to a general concern for teachers to provide their learners with opportunities to use language for communicative purposes; the latter more committed to stimulating the processes of language learning themselves through the language. There are certainly many synopses of the guiding principles of CLT to be found, and within these there are important differences. The following typical list of ten principles was offered by the main British national agency on language teaching and research, the Centre for Information on Language Teaching and Research (CILT):

1   Intention to Mean
2   Information Gap
3   Personalisation
4   Unpredictability
5   Legitimacy
6   Target Language Use
7   Approach to Error
8   Authenticity
9   Speech v. Writing
10   Practice v. Real Language

(CILT 1989)

What do these mean in practice?

Intention to mean relates to the way language nearly always has a 'meaning potential' (Halliday 1978) or function to fulfil in communicating an idea or purpose. Language is rarely used simply to provide practice of a structural model.

Information gap is the phrase that is used when there is a genuine exchange of information; in other words, there is a gap of information between two or more people which is bridged through language (text, aural material, etc.).

Personalisation describes how language is used to convey personal experiences and information. It can also relate to the way language is responded to in a personal sense; for example, making choices on the basis of information received, or reacting emotionally to its content.

Unpredictability describes the way that language input – whether printed or spoken – always includes unforeseen elements. Language is never wholly predictable.

Legitimacy of tasks or activities refers to the way language is used in the real world to operationalise real-life events. This is the whole purpose of language, and what makes it worthy of effort to acquire. It is perceived legitimacy which creates motivation to use language.

The status of the foreign language in the classroom indicates the extent to which the second language is used in the pedagogic context. Traditionally, in academic study of language, learning took place through discussion in English of discrete grammar points. Using a high degree of foreign language rests on the belief that exposure is central to the learning process.

Approach to error raises the question of when and how to correct. Error correction in language learning has traditionally been seen as a central pedagogic tool for the teacher. Questioning how effective this may be, or indeed when and how to correct, is based on the notion that tolerance of error may be more important in the long run as the learner constructs their internal language system at their own rate, not that prescribed by the teacher.

Authenticity of language describes how real-life materials (realia) are used as the basis of teaching and learning, not texts wholly fabricated with some didactic purpose in mind. The argument is that authenticity in language recreates the foreign culture in the classroom, enhances motivation and prepares for eventually living in the other environment.

Distinction between spoken and written language emphasises the important differences between the two forms. Studying written language does not necessarily provide a basis for oral competence, as many graduate students of foreign languages have discovered to their cost.

Practice versus real language draws attention to the fact that practice of structural forms is not the same as genuine, meaningful interactions in and through the language, and relates back to *intention to mean* and *legitimacy of tasks*.

It is easy to see how these pedagogic principles relate very closely to the mood of applied linguistics and the direction of methodological development described earlier in this chapter. Grammar is not mentioned in this list. Its presence is only implied, and then its role in learning a foreign language is perceived negatively. Practice for practice's sake, as in audio-lingualism, is out. What replaces these traditional pillars of language teaching is a naturalistic view of the learning process. On the face of it, there appears to be very little difference between what is described in the list above and the principles we might use to describe the process of learning a first language. Indeed, this form of communicative language teaching is seemingly constructed by analogy with first-language learning. The accent on the authentic and natural; the emphasis on meaning and linguistic exposure; the stress on letting the natural language-learning processes of the learner take their course.

We would not wish to misrepresent communicative language teaching, and, as referred to above, since its inception it has existed in many different forms. There are hard- and soft-liners in the extent to which grammar features in a communicative methodology and how. However, the spirit of CLT is captured in these ten principles, and, given they are supplied by the UK's leading national research and INSET (in-service education and training) support agency in modern languages, we must take them seriously. What did they look like in practice? In the next section, we see how CLT has been interpreted for application in classroom practice in British schools.

Curriculum reform

In his book on curriculum renewal in school foreign-language learning, John Clark (1987) draws a distinction between three broad systems in shaping teaching: classical humanism, reconstructionism and progressivism. The first classical tradition is based on intellectual capacities and insight into content and structure. It is linear in presentation and leads to skills of analysis, synthesis and aesthetic judgement. In the second case, reconstructionism is more sensitive to social function: ends and means. 'Good' habits and skills are acquired, and practical usefulness stressed; although the path for developing these is set by the teacher. The third 'progressive' system is much more learner-centred and aimed at promoting individual development. It is based on their communicative needs and aims to facilitate self-expression.

It is easy to interpret the methodological developments of past decades in these terms. The grammar–translation method can be set within the classical humanist tradition with its emphasis on knowledge for knowledge's sake. Audio-lingualism began a process of reconstruction which continues in CLT and points towards progressivism. But curriculum reform rarely develops in tandem alongside theoretical and methodological trends. If we step inside a time machine and go back to Britain in the early 1980s, we find modern languages in schools still in the grip of grammar–translation. The basis of this philosophy is enshrined in the O level: an examination set by university boards and very much reflecting their own academic preoccupations. As such, translation, from and to French, predominates; dictation is a measure of linguistic competence; oral skills form only a small percentage of the final marks awarded and written accuracy is at a premium. The subject of language content is wholly constructed from idealised forms and authentic materials are conspicuous by their absence. Audio-lingualism is at last waning, although its replacement, situational language learning, still isolates and practises grammar structures in a way which is depersonalising and demotivating.

However, reconstructionist forces are at work. In the Council of Europe a new style of foreign-language syllabus is being constructed. Known as the 'threshold level' (van Ek, 1975), this takes a different view of language and how it should be taught. Rather than placing the emphasis on the accumulated mastery of grammar, here the accent is on 'getting by' in the language in a range of pre-determined contexts. They take inspiration from Wilkins's (1976) notional–functional syllabuses where language-learning objectives are defined in terms of the pragmatic ends which can be served. Language is apportioned out; learners pass through a series of topic areas. These ideas meet with a 'bottom-up' movement formed by teachers themselves. Finding a large proportion of their pupils unable or unwilling to reach for the O-level heights, they construct a series of graded tests as a way of acknowledging progress as it occurs (Harding *et al.* 1980). Again, the topic matter is very functional. Pupils learn to get things done and carry on exchanges in the foreign language. These two undercurrents react with and respond to methodological advances in CLT in the world of English as a foreign language. Revolution occurs: GCSE.

The General Certificate of Secondary Education (GCSE) came about for many reasons, not least of which was the general educational aim of doing away with the two-tier system of General Certificate of Education (GCE) O level and Certificate of Secondary Education (CSE). In modern languages it provided a vehicle to put the advances of the past two decades into practice. It is worth recalling its guiding principles:

The aims of a course in French leading up to a GCSE examination should be;

2.1 to develop the ability to use French effectively for purposes of practical communication,

2.2 to form a sound base of the skills, language and attitudes required for further study, work and leisure,

2.3 to offer insights into the culture and civilisation of French-speaking countries,

2.4 to develop an awareness of the nature of language and language learning,

2.5 to provide enjoyment and intellectual stimulation,

2.6 to encourage positive attitudes to foreign language learning and to speakers of foreign languages and a sympathetic approach to other cultures and civilisations,

2.7 to promote learning skills of a more general application (e.g. analysis, memorising, drawing of inferences).

(DES 1985, p. 1)

Translation was out – so was dictation. In its place were the 'four skills': equal weighting was given to listening, speaking, reading and writing. Learning became pupil-centred as the notion of pupil as host and tourist was put centre stage in designing activities and preparing materials. Authentic materials were given a prominence hitherto unknown, and in place of accuracy there was tolerance to error and the notion of language which would be understandable to the sympathetic native speaker.

The first cohort of pupils took a GCSE exam in 1987. As we write in the late 1990s, it is still with us with very little modification. An element of coursework as part of the final assessment has been introduced, and for reasons of authenticity, rubrics in teaching and exam materials are now nearly exclusively given in the target language. For the most part, however, the format and content remain essentially unchanged. Of course, during this time, a second major revolution has taken place; that of the National Curriculum. The political thrust of the National Curriculum meant that its *raison d'être* was always more than didactic, as there were moves towards centralisation, prescription and control of what was taught in schools and how. For modern languages, it provided an opportunity to debate and discuss the structure and content of learning and teaching in an unprecedented manner. The present National Curriculum document of ten pages (DFE 1995) is a distillation of some five previous versions which have appeared since the 195-page Initial Advice (DES 1990). Later, we shall comment on some of the issues and ambiguities contained in these documents. For the moment, it is worth noting that many aspects of the National Curriculum remain in the GCSE mould which, indeed, it now subsumes. The four skills are here represented by the four 'Attainment Targets'; the host/tourist accent is defined, with an increased vocational element, in a set of 'Areas of Experience' which follow a similar line to the GCSE topics – everyday activities, personal and social life, the world around us, the world of work, the international world. 'Level Descriptions' apply for ages 11–14, while the GCSE A–G grades apply thereafter for ages 15–16. There is a more refined sense of progression. Figure 1.2 is an example of the speaking-attainment target descriptions. By mapping across the levels, it can be seen that progression is tracked in terms of: length of utterance; amount of support; conceptual familiarity; and linguistic accuracy/sophistication.

Various skills and understandings are also required in developing the use of the target language as the Programme of Study Part 1 indicates:

1 Communicating in the Target Language
  Pupils should be given opportunities to:

   (a) communicate with each other in pairs and groups and with their teacher;
   (b) use language for real purposes, as well as practice skills . . .

2 Language skills
  Pupils should be taught to:

   (a) listen attentively and listen for gist and detail;
   (b) follow instructions and directions . . .

3 Language-learning skills and knowledge of language
  Pupils should be taught to:

   (a) learn by heart phrases and short extract, e.g. rhymes, poems, songs, jokes, tongue twisters;
   (b) acquire strategies for committing familiar language to memory . . .

4 Cultural Awareness
  Pupils should be given opportunities to:

■ **Level 1**
Pupils respond briefly, with single words or short phrases, to what they see and hear. Their pronunciation may be approximate, and they may need considerable support from a spoken model and from visual cues.

■ **Level 2**
Pupils give short, simple responses to what they see and hear. They name and describe people, places and objects. They use set phrases for purposes such as asking for help and permission. Their pronunciation may still be approximate and the delivery hesitant, but their meaning is clear.

■ **Level 3**
Pupils take part in brief prepared tasks of at least two or three exchanges, using visual or other cues to help them initiate and respond. They use short phrases to express personal responses, such as likes, dislikes and feelings. Although they use mainly memorised language, they occasionally substitute items of vocabulary to vary questions or statements.

■ **Level 4**
Pupils take part in simple structured conversations of at least three or four exchanges, supported by visual or other cues. They are beginning to use their knowledge of language to adapt and substitute single words and phrases. Their pronunciation is generally accurate and they show some consistency in their intonation.

■ **Level 5**
Pupils take part in short conversations, seeking and conveying information and opinions in simple terms. They refer to recent experience and future plans, as well as everyday activities and interests. Although there may be some mistakes, pupils make themselves understood with little or not difficulty.

■ **Level 6**
Pupils initiate and develop conversations that include past, present and future actions and events. They are beginning to improvise and paraphrase. They use the target language to meet most of their routine needs for information and explanation. Although they may be hesitant at times, pupils make themselves understood with little or no difficulty.

■ **Level 7**
Pupils give and justify opinions when discussing matters of personal or topical interest. They adapt language to deal with some unprepared situations. They speak with good pronunciation and intonation. Their accuracy is such that they are readily understood.

■ **Level 8**
Pupils show increasing confidence in dealing with unpredictable elements in conversations, or with people who are unfamiliar. They discuss facts, ideas and experiences, using a range of vocabulary, structures and time references. They speak confidently with good pronunciation and intonation, and their language is largely accurate with few mistakes of any significance.

■ **Exceptional performance**
Pupils discuss a wide range of factual and imaginative topics, giving and seeking personal views and opinions in informal and formal situations. They speak fluently, with consistently accurate pronunciation, and show an ability to vary intonation. They give clear messages and make few errors.

Figure 1.2 National Curriculum in modern foreign languages

(a) work with authentic materials, including newspapers, magazines, books, films, radio, and television, from the countries or communities of the target language;

(b) come into contact with native speakers in the country and, where possible, abroad . . .

(DFE 1995, pp. 2–3)

Many aspects of the National Curriculum seem perfectly congruous with the principles of communicative language teaching discussed earlier in this chapter. It is therefore a pertinent question to ask if application of this methodology has led to dramatic improvement in the linguistic proficiency of secondary school pupils. Is this the case?

It is always difficult to assess real improvement, especially when we are not comparing like with like. From a recent report from the Office of Her Majesty's Inspectorate of School (OFSTED 1995) it is certain that more foreign-languages learning is taking place. National audits also show a small but continued rise in percentage passes in top grades at GCSE. Pupils seem more motivated, and classroom materials and activities have, apparently, never been more appealing, engaging and culturally authentic. However, all is not rosy, and distinct problems are also evident. The same OFSTED report offers evidence that achievement is generally higher at Key Stage 3 (age 11–14) than Key Stage 4 (15–16 years). Moreover, standards of achievement are better in years 7 and 8 (11–13) than year 9 (13–14). Certainly, there is more target language in the classroom, and pupils develop a good understanding of it. However, their normal classroom discourse is conducted in English, and few, it seems, are willing to speak the foreign language spontaneously or to take the initiative in attempting longer utterances. By Key Stage 4 (15–16 years) the apparent enthusiasm of beginner lessons has gone and progression from Key Stage 3 slows down markedly. The picture is one of progressing stagnation in language learning. Why is this so?

Of course, there are those who would argue that the reason is because there is not enough communicative language teaching in lessons. Certainly, it is difficult to equate the highly routinised practice of stock phrases in lessons with the naturalness apparent in CLT's approach. To coin a cliché, pupils are often 'walking phrase books' and spend most of their time ordering meals they are not going to eat, planning journeys they are not going to make, and speaking to and hearing about people they do not know. Indeed, it could be argued that much that goes on in the name of communicative language teaching in the average coursebook is just as repetitive as audio-lingualism, is just as contrived as situational language learning. The stress on transaction for contrived pragmatic purposes obscures the value of interaction on various psychological and social levels. No wonder, therefore, that enthusiasm wanes as the weight of phrases to remember gets ever heavier.

Others might argue that this is inevitable and inherent in communicative language teaching itself. They might point out that materials may be authentic but they are decontextualised in the classroom. Unpredictability is a fact of life, but not a natural pedagogic characteristic. Tasks may be legitimate to real life but lose their relevance among teachers and pupils. Genuine information gaps are rare. Imagination can only take you so far; about to the third year of foreign-language learning if the OFSTED report is to be believed. Finally, there are simply not the opportunities to mimic the exposure of real-life experience in the foreign language in the classroom where the majority of pupils are at the same rudimentary level and cannot supply models of good practice to each other. The teacher is not enough. This situation leads to a fundamental question: is it the application of CLT that is flawed or CLT itself?

As we have argued, it is not incontrovertibly true that the methodology implied in GCSE and the National Curriculum can be described as communicative language teaching at all. It does share many elements of the ten principles listed earlier. However, there is still much ambiguity over the role of grammar learning and the use of English in the foreign-language classroom. Take these two sets of statements. First:

> Much confusion arises from the use of the word grammar to refer to two quite different things: first, the framework of structures which form the skeleton of any language; secondly, the attempt to describe these structures in more or less formal terms, rarely using the target language. The latter is of very limited value to most pupils.
> . . . Learners of all abilities are much more likely to be able to grasp and work with grammatical structures if these are presented not through formal exposition but through demonstrations which make a strong visual or aural impression and require an active response.
>
> (DES 1990, pp. 121–2)

Now compare:

> An increasing awareness of (the framework of structures) can be an important ingredient in learners' progress towards a truly independent use of language. If learners can be helped to see the common features of the chunks of language which they have learnt, they will be better able to adapt them to the demands of different situations and increasingly to check their own understanding.
> . . . Teachers may nevertheless judge that a brief explanation in English would help, but such interventions should be short.
>
> (ibid.)

On the one hand, there is the apparent near 'Krashenite' need for exposure to the foreign language in order to supply lots of comprehensible input from which pupils induce grammar. On the other, insight is needed, which may be supplied from explicit technical explanations. Where is the balance to be struck? Is not the message that target language is good, English is bad; induction is best, deduction is limited? In other words, it is all too easy to go through the motions of communicative language teaching in a way that makes a caricature of its original aims. This argument leads us back to the type of fundamental questions which were set out at the start of this chapter: what is it to know a language? What is the relationship between first and second-language processes? How is learning connected to acquiring language? What value is there in learning materials?

Some would claim that communicative language teaching skews what might be done methodologically in the answers it comes up with in response to these questions. Writers as far back as Palmer in the early part of this century to the present day have been at pains to point out that you have to separate out learning from knowing or using. In other words, what communicative language teaching is describing is competence or proficiency not the means to acquiring it. It seems the National Curriculum itself is prone to this assumption in that its Programme of Study Part 1 does collapse a list of desirable skills under a title which includes both *learning* and *using*. It is as if using skills is the means to learning them, and learning is the means to their use. Clearly, this is a circular argument which fails to prioritise or order the processes involved for pedagogic purposes. This has resulted in some polarisation of opinion. First, the 'return to grammar' movement, the advocates of which have seen CLT as misguided all along. The solution is to bring back grammar, which is seen as being more effective for pupils' *learning*. Second, there are those who believe that what we lack is the right conditions, the right amount of time and the right materials. Individuals in this movement are forever on the look-out for more and more imaginative materials and motivating classroom activities. The fundamental message behind this book is that both extremes are misguided: one yearns for an idealised version of the past, the other seeks to find an idealised vision of the future. What we intend to present here is a methodological third way, but this first requires us to go back to examine some of the theoretical premises of language and language teaching and learning. This is the topic of the next chapter.

Conclusion

This chapter has set a background context to the book. We have briefly referred to the way applied linguistics and teaching methodologies have evolved this century and their characteristics in recent decades. The relationship between theory and practice has been highlighted, as well as the connections between modern-languages teaching and learning and English as a foreign language. The principles and justification for communicative language teaching have been presented in detail and their application within the British context discussed. How communicative language teaching has influenced curricular developments has also been documented. Finally, the results of almost two decades of reform have been examined along with possible explanations for methodological disappointments. Particular shortcomings have been commented upon in the light of possible limitations in the application of CLT in its present form and inherent difficulties of CLT itself. In the next chapter, we shall return to theoretical and pedagogic issues and move towards a presentation of the conceptual thinking which underlies and justifies our focus on learning strategies.

2 What it is to know, what it is to learn

Introduction

In the last chapter we looked at the development of language-teaching methodologies over the last century or so and discussed the ways that research and thinking about the nature of language connected to these. We concluded with some consideration of communicative language teaching: the methodology which has perhaps most dominated classrooms in recent decades. We made the point that much of the general approach to communicative language teaching resonated with various key aspects of applied linguistic research in ways which made oral-based, meaning-focused teaching perfectly congruous with them; albeit that there were theoretical differences of opinion between researchers and methodologists. In the early days of communicative language teaching, the need and inspiration for a different teaching methodology came from a response to various sociocultural and pedagogic factors rather than an applied science in itself. However, since its inception, the two have grown closer together and now it is normal to think of methodological developments in terms of the under-pinning models of language learning implicit in them. This chapter takes this discussion forward and looks further at how we think about language and learning. We shall connect this with the notion of linguistic progression enshrined in the British National Curriculum as one attempt to put learning theory into practice. We shall also refer to a developing sense of the 'competent' language learner. All this is a prelude to considering learning strategies *per se*. Here we shall look at the way they can be defined and conceived, as well as the models of learning they suggest. Our discussion deals with popular taxonomies of strategies and what these may look like in practice. In particular, we are concerned with individual differences in strategy use. Finally, we return to questions of pedagogy: the importance that strategies may have in the classroom and how this has shaped some recent thinking about curriculum design. This chapter provides a theoretical framework and justification for the practical and theoretical content of the rest of the book, and cross-referencing will be used throughout to connect the various strands of our discussion.

Knowing a language

In the last chapter, we raised a number of questions including 'what it is to know' a language. We showed how the notion of 'competence' has formed a core idea to conceptualising linguistic progress. Communicative competence has been used by such writers as Hymes, Canale and Swain and Bachman to categorise the various social, cognitive and linguistic elements involved in being able to communicate with others. And, of course, behind this notion, there is the Chomskyan idea of innate competence, as opposed to skill-based behaviourism, with all that may or may not imply in terms of second-language-learning potential.

Clearly, what is at stake may be termed 'orders of knowledge' of language; that is, in the way it is conceived and represented. For example, what is involved in thinking of language as an innate characteristic of the mind is very different from seeing it as a process of skill acquisition. The first involves natural biological processing; the second, habit-forming practice. As suggested in Chapter 1, these understandings are bound to give rise to different pedagogic assumptions when it comes to designing classroom teaching. This statement seems true and to be the implicit justification for the explosion which has taken place over recent decades in research into second-language acquisition. The hunt is on, it seems, to discover how languages are learned so that we might know how best to teach them. This hunt has given rise to its own factions, disciplines and approaches in attempting to capture what language is and what it is to know it. Each of these approaches have also produced their own vocabulary, or language, to talk about language. We saw some of these in Chapter 1 in dealing with communicative competence and some of the psychological theories of language running in parallel to them. Here are some others which have, if only for brief periods, had their advocates:

Dichotomies in theory

Skill getting v. Skill using (Rivers and Temperley 1978)
Usage v. Use (Widdowson 1978)
Conscious v. Unconscious (Lantolf and Frawley 1983)
Formal v. Informal (Krashen and Seliger 1976)
Controlled v. Automatic (Shiffrin and Schneider 1977)
Learning v. Acquisition (Krashen 1982)
Analysed v. Unanalysed (Bialystok 1984)
Accuracy v. Fluency (Brumfit 1984)
Planned v. Unplanned (Ellis 1990)
Declarative v. Procedural (Anderson 1983)
Pre-communicative v. Communicative (Littlewood 1981)
CALPS v. BICS (Cognitive Academic Language Proficiency v. Basic Interpersonal Communication Skills) (Johnstone, 1989)

There is not the space here to go into each of these. Neither is it necessary. We offer them to give a flavour of what we above called 'orders of knowledge' in thinking about language. There are clearly many differences in the items listed. A few will preoccupy us increasingly in the later parts of this chapter. However, what they all share is an attempt to describe something of the underlying processes of language. Even without going into detail, it is clear from a common sense knowledge of language what many of these must mean. So, for example, Shiffrin and Schneider see a distinction to be made between controlling language, in a conscious way, and automatic use, which comes naturally. This notion seems to connect with the dichotomies between planned and unplanned, or conscious and unconscious and, arguably, some of the others in the list. In fact, we might see the list as a diversity of ways of drawing a distinction, to a greater or lesser extent, between explicit knowledge of language and implicit fluent use. Clearly, they cannot all be equally right; and yet, they cannot all be wrong either. There is sufficient overlap between them all which suggests a fundamental issue at stake. What is it?

Maybe behind these theoretical dichotomies is nothing more than the age-old question of formally expressed grammar knowledge and its apparent operation in practice. We saw in Chapter 1 how problematic a notion like grammar can be. There are many grammars in a single language, let alone across languages. And how do all these connect with the Chomskyan notion of 'Universal Grammar'? We also know that 'knowing a grammar' is not the same as 'knowing a language'. An analogy or two may be useful here. Let us suppose that being able to drive a car was simply the result of being told how to do it. It must then take only a matter of minutes to describe the dashboard, what each control does, and the operation of gears, brakes and accelerator. Yet, before anyone can drive, we all know it is a lot more complicated than that: there is a question of coordination, of a myriad of items left out in any 'expert's' description, and of individual responses to an infinite number of changing road conditions. We have also all experienced the frustration of giving road directions to someone, who subsequently becomes hopelessly lost. Why? One reason is that in our description we make all sorts of assumptions and do not include items of knowledge which seem obvious to us but are not known to the novice. In other words, we do not always 'know' what we 'know'. We therefore have difficulty passing it onto others. Language is a bit like that. We all know our first language, but most do not know what this knowing is: how it works. Even if we are competent in second or third languages, we are apt to forget how we learned them, and may not know what we do to make them work. Applied linguists have spent a considerable amount of time and money in making this knowledge explicit, with the result that we now know more about what it is to know. However, it is clear that there is perhaps still more that we do not know and, that for much of our time in language teaching, we are hopelessly trying to match our speedy driving instructor who can tell you all you need to know in a matter of minutes – who can *tell* you, but do you learn?

Clearly, the writers behind the dichotomies listed above have reached this realisation and have attempted to go beyond a simple instruction-to-learn model.

We can see that beneath such notions as control, there is a plethora of linguistic features – phonetic, phonological, morphological, syntactical and semantic – to be dealt with. Similarly, in the conscious, analysed planning which may go on in order to operate language, not only are all these linguistic elements involved, but also a whole lot of metalinguistic and paralinguistic aspects concerned with the social context in which the language is occurring, not to mention the thoughts, feelings and intentions of the individuals involved. All of these features have to be managed – at once! – for language and communication to happen successfully.

It is also clear that the dichotomies suggest some sort of opposition between those on the right and those on the left-hand sides of the list. Those items on the left-hand side are all about the means to the end of language competence. Here are to be found all the conscious, explicit, controlled learning processes. On the other side of the list are notions connected with competence: fluency, automatic, use. The latter are good. The former are bad, but still offer the necessary means to get there. Such an image is misleading. In a sense, even in our first language, we are continually encountering situations which require us to draw on some of the features of the left-hand side of the list. Similarly, most of these are never completely learned but undergo a continuous process of development. Perhaps it is better to think of each of them as a continuum, with a particular language user travelling between them at any one point in time and, indeed, in any one particular linguistic utterance. Still, even if this is true, we need to recognise that both sides of the list do undergo development or growth. In other words, linguistic progression is implied by this sort of list. Presumably, individual language users do have, at any one point in time of their linguistic development, more or less competence in each. Such elements as fluency and unplanned language use must therefore be quantifiable. Similarly, pedagogic planning needs to take such development into account in its curriculum design and classroom methodology. Let us examine a linguistic case in point: the National Curriculum for Modern Foreign Languages in England to which we referred in Chapter 1.

In keeping with many teaching–learning programmes, language is divided up into the four basic skill areas, here designated the attainment targets: listening; speaking; reading; writing. Less conventionally, each of these is then divided up into eight levels of attainment. The descriptions for each of these levels make explicit the elements of progression envisaged. The strands of progression across each attainment target can be expressed in terms of three basic areas:

1   Length/type/form of language

    • Formal/informal
    • Style
    • Grammatical sophistication and accuracy
    • Content

2   Familiarity of language

    • Degree of unpredictability
    • Need for improvisation

3   Level of support

- Visual clues
- Cognates
- Gesture
- Written clues

These features can be traced across the four attainment targets and the level descriptions. For example, levels 1 and 2 listening require understanding of short, familiar statements which may need lots of support. Levels 6 and 7 require comprehension of longer, unfamiliar passages with little support. Productive skills such as writing parallel this model. In levels 1 and 2, familiar language in the form of short words and phrases is copied; while levels 6 and 7 ask for more independence in producing longer, unfamiliar passages in response to un-predictable contexts. Grammatical accuracy and sophistication also run across these levels and targets: for example, active recognition of past, present and future tenses is stipulated for level 5 in listening and reading; and productively for speaking and writing at level 6.

In the Programme of Study Part 1 of the National Curriculum, progression in learning and using the target language is itemised under such headings as: communicating in the target language; language skills; language-learning skills and knowledge of language; cultural awareness. Taken together with the attainment targets and level descriptions, we have here an intended picture of progression in modern languages which moves pupils to a higher level of competence in the types of linguistic, social and cultural skills we have discussed above. Moreover, it implies that the development of a set of language-learning skills is necessary for continued linguistic progress. A greater degree of independence on the part of the language learner is also implied, and it is to this feature that we now wish to turn.

Autonomy

Much of what we have described and discussed thus far can be seen as thinking through some of the issues at stake in comparing the processes of first and second-language learning. We have suggested that communicative language teaching itself is predicated on a conceptual analogy between the naturalness in all processes of language learning, whether first or second. The models of learning set out show dichotomies between the route to becoming proficient in a language and actual competence in that language. The dimension of independence or autonomy is central to this view of language. These days, autonomy has very many applications and implications, many of them social, political and cultural. There are indeed arguments for regarding the rights to autonomy of learners in all educational settings. Such a discussion would need to consider the philosophy of language and its tendency to restrict as well as empower learners caught up within educational discourses. Issues of social class, gender and race would come into such a discussion, as well as the mechanisms of authority within pedagogic contexts. Much of this is, however, outside the scope of this book. Here, we are more interested in the role that autonomy may play within language learning and teaching.

Autonomy is at the heart of first-language learning, in that acquiring a language is *the* process by which every one of us establishes existence as an independent personality. Until this occurs we are dependent on others to define our relationship to the world and navigate through it for us. In acquiring language, we learn to do this decision making for ourselves and to express what is our own individuality. This cannot be the case when we learn our second, third or more languages. By then, we are more or less formed individuals, subject, of course, to growth and development in the response to life's experiences. We already have a language with which we can mediate ourselves in the world. A second language is not, strictly speaking, needed. However, many aspects of language learning still need a degree of autonomy to be successful. For example, in order to be competent, we need to be able to act on our own outside of the pedagogic context. To redefine ourselves and our relationship to the world in a second-language context, we must function independently in that language. This involves our own substantive choices about what is to be done and said. It also requires our own responses. This statement may seem to be obvious. But a moment's consideration will show how much of language classroom activity has been anything but individually focused in this way. Even in the communicative classroom, rehearsal of interactional dialogues set in the restaurant, post office or cinema leaves out much of this individual choice, restricting decisions to a few non-consequential alternatives. Moreover, most language learners will already have a relatively sophisticated personality, but this will not be developed in their second language. It is necessary to find the linguistic ways and means to express this identity in second-language contexts. How will this come about if most language lessons are based around analysis of grammar, practice drills or even idealised communicative dialogues? Real language is messy and instantly responsive to the moment. Here, the individuals involved have the space to express who they are and these responses necessarily entail aspects of autonomy. We are not claiming that anyone can do or say whatever they want. We are arguing, however, that real language occurs between independent individuals.

We do not want to become ensnared in the controversy which equates first with second-language acquisition, or which overstresses the dichotomy between what has been called rehearsal and performance. Both debates gravitate towards simplistic idealisations of opposing views. What we are claiming is that the dimension of autonomy is so fundamental to the nature of language that successful learning cannot occur without it being present in some degree. In brief, it is inconceivable that someone can develop communicative competence, in any of the features mentioned above, and not also be operating increasingly within their own semi-independent social, psychological and linguistic-generating structures. If this is not the case, then they will merely be performing what others have instructed them to do. Good language learning is about increasing autonomy. In fact, we would go as far as to argue that someone cannot be a successful language learner and not also be an autonomous language learner and, hence, user. One important consequence of this line of argument is then to ask to what extent autonomy exists in any particular pedagogic context and, more specifically, in what ways is it planned for?

We have approached this discussion through a general consideration of autonomy and the development of an individual through their first language. We have also thought about the element of autonomy in second-language-learning contexts. Here, it tends to have a much more narrow definition. Little (1994) sums it up as follows:

> Learner autonomy entails acceptance of responsibility for one's learning. This means:
>
> • establishing a personal agenda for learning;
> • taking at least some of the initiatives that shape the learning process;
> • developing the capacity to evaluate the extent and success of one's learning.

Of course, this definition focuses on formal learning processes rather than deep psychological mechanisms of developing linguistic competence. We would go one step further and argue that introducing explicit elements of autonomy into any formulation of learning is a prerequisite to moving towards independent language competence in the latter. Autonomy does not then mean do-it-yourself language teaching or encourage a get-rid-of-the-teacher response. Rather we see it as a necessary condition of developing linguistic competence; one which operates in interpenetrable forms between pedagogic and cognitive processes. We presume that this is what the successful language learner does, more or less on their own, in acquiring competence. The rest of this chapter, and indeed book, explores these notions of autonomy and learning strategy both theoretically, from an action research perspective, and in terms of their practical implementation. We want to approach our own theoretical perspective and the framework it provides for understanding learning strategies through a consideration of the 'good' language learner.

The good language learner and the notion of strategy

The 'good language learner' research tradition is now well over 20 years old. It is predicated on a simple distinction: what is it that successful language learners do which unsuccessful ones do not? And behind this basic question is a pedagogic realisation that if we can find out what good language learners do, then maybe we can tell the other learners in order to improve their chances. Of course, we now know that the ambition to catalogue what the good learner does and then train others in these skills is not quite as easy as it may seem. In fact, it is not always easy to know what the good language learner is doing. They may not know it themselves, and therefore will be unable to tell you. Similarly, it is not a straight forward matter to get inside the 'black box' of the human brain and see what is going on. As in much applied linguistic research and investigations into the processes of second-language acquisition, we are mostly left to surmise underlying process from surface product; beyond this we often simply do not know. Later, we shall also discuss how there are considerable individual differences in language learning: what works for one does not work for another. In short, there is no single type of 'good language' learner but many variations each with their own characteristics, techniques and approaches.

Nevertheless, good-language-learner research has told us much in a formal way which we did not know before. In a seminal study in 1975, Stern drew up a list of ten strategies used by the good language learner:

1 Planning strategy
2 Active strategy
3 Empathetic strategy
4 Formal strategy
5 Experimental strategy
6 Semantic strategy
7 Practice strategy
8 Communication strategy
9 Monitoring strategy
10 Internalisation strategy

The list was drawn from his own thinking about the nature of linguistic competence and his response to three perennial problems of second-language acquisition: 'the disparity between the inevitable and deep-seated presence of the first language (and other languages previously learned) as a reference system and the inadequate ... development of the new language as a new reference system' (Stern 1975); the code-communication problem where the learner has to find a way of dealing with both the linguistic forms and the messages to be conveyed; and the 'choice between rational and intuitive learning' (see Naiman *et al.* 1978/1996) – in other words, the balance between learning 'by feel' and learning according to an objective decision about the best way to go about it. This conceptual list gave rise to a classic study, *The Good Language Learner* (ibid.), which set about cataloguing these various strategies, what they looked like in practice, on the basis of collected data.

At this point, and since this is the first time in the book that the word 'strategy' has been employed as a central part to the discussion, it is worth pausing to consider its meaning. A dictionary definition of strategy refers to 'a clever plan or method; the art of employing plans towards achieving a goal' (*Longman Concise English Dictionary* (1985), p. 1377). From this definition, it is easy to adapt and apply this sense to a learning context: a learning strategy becomes the means to achieving the goal of linguistic competence, the plan or method. Since these early studies from Stern and Naiman *et al.*, others have developed conceptual notions of language-learning strategies defined as:

strategies that contribute to the development of the language system which the learner constructs and affect learning directly;

(Wenden and Rubin 1987, p. 23)

the special thoughts and behaviours that individuals use to help them comprehend, learn, or retain new information;

(O'Malley and Chamot 1990, p. 1)

steps taken by students to enhance their own learning;

(Oxford 1990, p. 1)

specific actions, behaviours, steps, or techniques that students employ – often consciously – to improve their progress in internalizing, storing, retrieving, and using the L2.

(Oxford 1993, p. 175)

Encapsulated in these definitions are various dimensions of learning which it would be perfectly possible to unpick if required. Similarly, from Stern's list above it is easy to construct the 'ideal-type' good language learner. They are above all someone who is active on a number of fronts. They like to communicate with others (communication strategy) and are tolerant and outgoing with native speakers of the language they are learning (empathetic strategy). They plan according to a personal learning style (planning strategy) and practise willingly (practice strategy). They do have a technical know-how concerning language (formal strategy) and develop an increasingly separate mental system in which they are able to think ideas in the foreign language (internalisation strategy) and search for meaning (semantic strategy). At the same time, although they are methodical in approach, they are willing to be flexible and constantly look to revise their linguistic understandings (experimental strategy). Finally, they are self-aware, go out of their way to be active in language learning (active strategy), and are able to assess their performance critically in language use (monitoring strategy).

These strategies, perhaps unsurprisingly, do demonstrate the various levels, dimensions or elements in language learning: the social context; the learning element; the interactional nature; the cognitive skills; the level of awareness. We all recognise something of ourselves in this list, and something of the good learners we have worked with. Yet, we also know that these strategies rarely exist as a complete set for learners as they develop their linguistic competence. Here, we are up against the problem that was raised earlier in the book, namely, describing the end product is not the same as prescribing the means to get there. We certainly know that simply describing these strategies to a learner with examples is likely to be no more successful than describing grammar and expecting them to generate fluent language on the basis of that knowledge. As in the car analogy above, knowing is one thing and doing is another. We will encounter practical illustrations of the difference in Chapter 5. Nevertheless, the list does enable us to reflect on some important aspects of the nature of strategies and their use:

1   Do strategies refer to the actual processes involved in language manipulation or the study skills necessary for organising learning: are they linguistic or academic?
2   Do learning strategies refer to naturally induced habits in processing a second language or to taught behaviours and techniques: namely acquisition or learning?
3   Do strategies involve explicit knowledge of their use, reflection and pre-planning, or are they more automatic: are they conscious or intuitive?

We pose them as dichotomies, as either/or questions, although in many senses strategies are both. Certainly, subsequent learning-strategy research has dealt with these various foci to a greater or lesser extent. For example, Rubin (1975) used learner diaries with higher-education language learners to catalogue how they organise their thinking about language. Wong Fillmore (1979), on the other hand, studied the behaviour and practices of a young learner in a new native-language environment. These studies revealed two different aspects of strategy use. The first was able to show all the academic study skills mature language learners may have: how they memorise words and grammar; how meaning is induced from guessing and inferencing and the role that deductive reasoning will have in this process; how problems are solved and doubts verified; the ways in which they monitor their performance at different linguistic levels. The second demonstrated what it is to be an active language learner when plunged into a new linguistic situation: how joining in is important; how to make use of others, especially closest friends; and how impression management is all – if you act as if you understand, eventually, by employing a whole set of communication and discourse strategies, you will.

Here, it is worth also noting that the study of *communication strategies* has arisen as a whole distinct strand of research. Communication strategies are the means which learners have at their disposal to make sense in face-to-face exchanges and cope with breakdowns in communication; the strategic competence in Chapter 1. An important aspect in understanding and being understood, for example, may be the degree to which the learner can 'control' the dialogue by slowing it down and making use of intonation to seek further elucidation of particular elements within it (see Bialystok 1990). We shall refer to communication strategies in Chapters 3 and 4 in our discussion of how learners operate when speaking.

It is easy to apply the early work on learning strategies to the issues of learning and teaching, and the importance of autonomy, discussed earlier. We now know that a 'good' language learner is one who takes personal decisions, in an implicit or explicit manner, regarding what to do to facilitate learning in whatever context they find themselves. They know what to focus on and which strategies might apply at any particular stage of the learning experience. They actively seek information, opportunities to practise, and assistance from available resources, including people around them and from printed documentation. This description presupposes an individual development plan which, in many respects, is self-determined. The implication of this realisation is that lessons and teaching which are mostly directed by the teacher who chooses what is to be learned, when and how, run counter to this form of individualised linguistic development rather than enhancing it. In other words, many of the characteristics of the good language learner are discouraged rather than promoted in a teacher-centred language classroom. Little surprise, consequently, if progress and attainment are eventually modest.

The last statement is a broad generalisation; it is not possible to tar every classroom, deemed 'non-autonomous', with the same brush. And, as we saw in Chapter 1, there are vastly different methodologies and approaches to pedagogy in language learning. How do they each measure up? We will leave that question mostly in the air. Clearly, grammar–translation, with its prescribed route through the technicalities of syntax, does little by way of the list of ten strategies on page 37. But is the communicative classroom any better? There is the intention here to provide real meaning and personalised response. However, much that goes on in the name of such principles might, on closer inspection, appear similarly prescriptive and lacking in those very elements (genuine meaning and individual response) which it claims to be promoting. It is perhaps enough to repeat our cliché from Chapter 1, that many secondary school language learners spend most of their time ordering meals they are not going to eat, planning journeys they are not going to make and responding to people they will never meet. This accusation is a harsh one, but contains more than a grain of truth. It is startling to suppose that what is effective as an organisational principle for teaching in the classroom may actually inhibit active learning. In fact, the whole of this book is predicated on the belief that communicative language teaching, as we often know it in the context of the secondary school, has not delivered the linguistic goods precisely because an oversimplistic view of pedagogic implications has been adopted: one where the learner is left out in the cold. In the second part of this book, we shall discuss how others have gone about rectifying part of the problem through working with learning strategies. We shall discuss how learners might be trained in strategy use and the consequences for pedagogy. First, however, we want to explore strategies themselves a little more.

We started this chapter by looking at the way others have tried to conceptualise the processes of learning a language. We argued that it is important to understand learning before the implications for teaching can be realised. In our brief consideration of the good-language-learner research tradition and the place of strategies in this we again saw how various dimensions were grouped: social, academic, cognitive. So far these have remained unconnected, and researchers have been content to describe what they think is going on with learners. All this does still beg the question of how the dimensions are connected in the totality of language learning? We now want to discuss possible underlying processes to these various strategies by again considering what we earlier called different 'orders of knowledge', and to do this with reference to one learning theory in particular; namely, cognitive theory.

Different orders of knowledge and the problem of knowing a language

Throughout the discussion so far we have referred on occasion to 'different orders of knowledge' when exploring the various dimensions of language learning and teaching. We have also posed the question: what is it to know a language? In Chapter 1 we saw how a linguistic watershed took place when theorists started to consider the innateness of language process as opposed to the behaviourist model. In this chapter we have looked at other dichotomies which attempt to capture something of the continua learners seem to move between in developing linguistic competence. And we have connected this discussion with notions of autonomy in language learning and the types of strategies which may be available to learners. What does all this add up to?

Clearly, knowing a language involves complex psychological processes, many of which seem to be beyond researcher observation. Learning a second language calls upon these, but not in an identical way from when the first language is learned. The second language has to sit alongside and/or integrate with the first. When an individual learns their first language it is bound up with the development of their cognitive maturity, and their very identity. This formed personality is brought to the second-language-learning process and has to be expressed within it. Some degree of autonomy must be present in this expression if someone is to be a competent language user, as this implies independence and choice in what is said and how. And the sorts of strategies we have listed also draw attention to the deep psychological as well as the social in language learning.

Knowing a language is obviously an extremely complex activity. Even at the fundamental levels of language – phonetics, phonology, morphology, and syntax – considerable control has to be exerted to be able to operationalise these effectively all at the same time. The simplest expression itself already demands manipulation of sound and organisation of structure. However, this is only the beginning of language, because, of course, all these sounds and structures also have to convey meanings. Semantic sense has also to be controlled in language in order for it to be effective. Both are highly problematic: ideas have to be understood and expressed; the language which carries these ideas has to be managed. And, of course, beyond the basic mechanics of the language there is a whole world of social and cultural dimensions which also have to be dealt with appropriately, and this with respect to the individual identity involved.

It is probably worth pausing to consider some of the key words used in the preceding paragraph: identity; control; problem. The sense we wish to convey behind this discussion is not of a language learner learning a language in some decontextualised, idealised realm disconnected from the problems and processes of everyday life, but quite the opposite: of someone plunged into the maelstrom of the world with its demands and mixed messages. Language is the medium with which individuals navigate their own particular path through life; it mediates our position at any one time and gets things done for us. It therefore helps us to control who we are and the social demands put upon us. It solves problems and is the principal means by which we express our identity to others and develop as individuals.

In this discussion, we can again identify the social and psychological dimensions – the orders of knowledge. At the same time, it is possible to see how these may operate at an explicit or implicit level, and at different times and places according to the requirements of particular contexts. The thrust and character of this discussion is in fact a very close parallel to that of the cognitive theorists.

A dictionary definition of cognition states that it is: 'the act or process of knowing that involves the processing of information and includes perception, awareness and judgement' (*Longman Concise English Dictionary* 1985), p. 267). Knowledge in this sense is 'information' to be processed. The whole area of cognitive psychology, and indeed the cognitive theoretical approach to language is much broader and larger than can be dealt with in the scope of this chapter. However, it is immediately possible to see how this perspective connects with our discussion so far: it is not so much that the orders of knowledge or dichotomies to which we refer occur as separate processes, but that they are all different forms of information being processed. The assumption is that no matter how distinct different aspects of language may be, they are all dealt with according to basic cognitive processes.

Modern day cognitive theorists have a lot in common with the Vygotskian tradition of psycholinguistics. Vygotsky was a Russian psychologist who died in 1934. However, after the translation into English of his seminal book, *Thought and Language* in 1962, his ideas have become increasingly influential in shaping thinking about language and learning. As the title of his book suggests, Vygotsky was particularly interested in the relationship between thinking and language, especially in the development of a child's first language. Famously, he argued that nothing appears at an *intra*-psychological level without first appearing at an *inter*-psychological level. In other words, the social plane of group discourse into which a child is plunged provides the conceptual schemes of thought to develop ideas and the means to express them. Not surprisingly, this does not occur overnight but takes years to develop. In the process, the individual's social positioning and conditioning also takes place: and language is the medium through which this happens.

Control is again a key notion from this perspective, as the mediation is very much about social control: of the world, of others and of oneself as a socially integrated individual. Each of these are 'problematic' relationships as they require balance or a sense of equilibrium in the way they connect to and affect the individual. Vygotsky saw that these problems were 'talked through' in language with the early learner. Piaget too had remarked on what was termed 'egocentric speech'; in other words, the talk which young language learners involve themselves in, but which is not addressed to another but themselves. This talk, often babble, was talk aimed at thinking through these problems and solving them. The articulate expression of speech itself creates a distance, an objective 'other', which facilitates thinking; in this case, in relationship to the world. Piaget thought this egocentric speech died away in the fully socialised mature child. However, Vygotsky believed it was internalised, where it acted as a kind of linguistic superego commenting on language and thought when it was employed in the self's controlled mediation of the world. Interestingly, it can still be called upon in an explicitly articulated form when problems become so great that they have to be externalised to be objectified and acted upon. We are perhaps all familiar with the plumber or mechanic who 'talks himself through' the possible range of problems when doing a repair. This talk seems to be an aid to thinking. Latter-day counselling techniques also seem to share something of this 'thinking out loud' as a way of controlling; not as an imposition but as a process of mediation. What has all this to do with learning a modern foreign language?

We have pointed out that the second-language learner in whom we are interested in the context of this book is a developed personality. However, this is not the case in the foreign language. In other words, they may have mature personality in L1, but there is still the need to express this identity in L2, and to find the linguistic means to do it. The L2 learner is thrust into an 'unknown' linguistic environment. Ideas have to be expressed there, and ideas can be found there. Moreover, the means to express these can also be found there. Finally, the whole learning experience is, as we have already said, problematic, so that developing a linguistic competence is very much about mediating, or control with respect to the world (the language to express and direct it), others (the language to understand and develop relationships) and self (to express what one needs to say about oneself and how to act).

A cognitive theoretical approach to second-language learning takes all this as information to be processed. At the same time, it understands that there are fundamental differences in the elements of what it is to know. The example of the differences between an explicit knowledge of how to drive a car and a practical know-how graphically illustrates the point. Let us take another example: making a cup of coffee. Presumably, we all know how to make a cup of coffee; probably, we were all once taught. In an early Vygotskian stage of language and thought development, all the objects in the sequence would have to be named. Next the order of the sequence would have to be set. Once these objects are named and the sequence adopted, the whole process becomes automatic: we do not make coffee by naming cups, kettles and spoons and then telling ourselves what we have to do. This 'proceduralising' seems to be a natural part of human psychology. There seems to be a need to proceduralise or automatise as much as possible. The process clears short-term memory for more immediate and new information which is always the most problematic. That which is now processed or 'known' is called up from long-term memory when need be. Whatever the information – social, cultural or basically linguistic – this is the cognitive principle by which the information is handled.

This discussion leads us to our first fundamental conceptual pairing in dealing with cognitive theory: *declarative* and *procedural* knowledge.

In his ACT (adaptive control of thinking) model, Anderson (1983, 1985) describes 'declarative' knowledge as propositional, conceptual knowledge which is stored as structural relationships. It is the things we know – the capital of France, or the notion of appropriacy. Often it is learned in an explicit manner, but is always passed to long-term memory where it is accessed on the basis of stimulus and input. It can be analysed if need be, that is, explicitly called to mind and operated upon. 'Procedural' knowledge, on the other hand, is unanalysed, automatic knowledge of how to do things. It is this knowledge which underlies the numerous cognitive skills we have in solving a multitudinous number of everyday problems. Some such knowledge, for example, deep linguistic knowledge in our first language, is only ever procedural – we do not 'know' what we are doing. Other knowledge, for example, musical scales, might start out being declarative – it is 'declared' to us – but then becomes proceduralised in the course of our use of it. What has all this to do with second language learning?

Figure 2.1 is one way to conceptualise language according to differences between declarative and procedural knowledge. On the vertical axis, we have placed established features of language, from basic phonetic articulation to its meta- and paralinguistic levels. On the horizontal axis we have placed declarative and procedural knowledge, being the two fundamental forms of information processing. A, B, C and D are indicated as *placings* in linguistic processing. At its simplest level, we might see that a mature native speaker of language operates at the far right of the diagram; as all linguistic levels are proceduralised. The most formal form of language-learning operates at the extreme left; where all levels are explicitly articulated and 'learned'. However, there is more that we can do with this diagram. One possibility would be to map particular language-learning activities into particular areas. For example, focus on grammar locates the activities along the vertical axis. There is the question as to whether the pedagogic strategy aims for deduction (declarative knowledge) or induction (developing procedural knowledge). It is also possible to locate any one individual's particular linguistic competence on this diagram. For example, someone may be operating in area B at a near native-speaker-like level, but not have 'proceduralised' all the basic linguistic information, that is, they have an accent. Finally, we would want to say that such a mapping is a way of offering possibilities only. It would be strange indeed if it were static. Rather, each element is constantly in flux as the learner develops, and this in response to the particular linguistic demands of the moment. In other words, what will be procedural in one linguistic context may be declarative in another. This possibility follows on from our previous point that things become more declarative when problems arise and we will see an example in relation to one of the case studies in Chapter 3.

Our route to understanding how this connects with learning strategies is to consider our other fundamental pair of concepts: *cognitive* and *metacognitive*.

We have already discussed how cognition might be defined as virtually any mental manipulation of information. Similarly, cognitive strategies can be understood as mental engagement with language in materials or tasks in order to develop understanding and hence learning. Cognitive strategies act *on* language

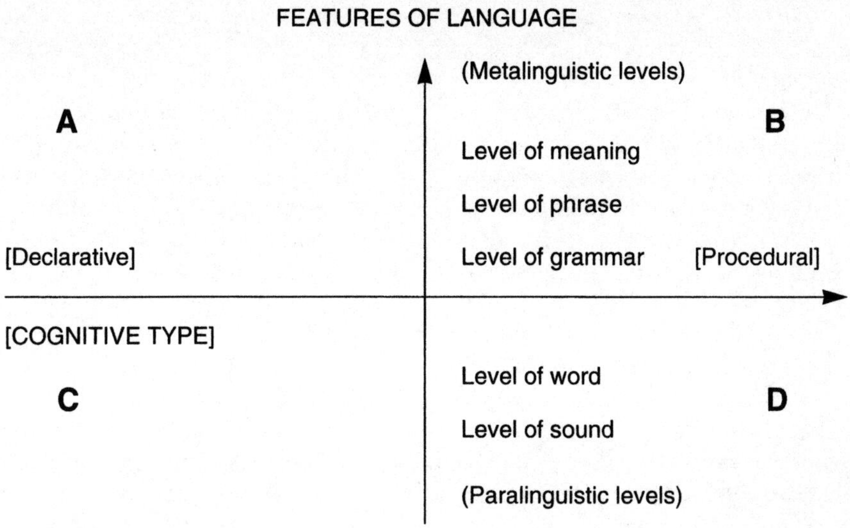

FEATURES OF LANGUAGE

Figure 2.1 Conceptualising language according to linguistic features and cognitive type

in the acquisition process and may be specifically involved in production of language. Detailed examples can be found in Chapter 4 and include: guessing at meaning on the basis of associated linguistic clues, or using imagery and repetition as part of memorisation strategies. Cognitive strategies also include many academic and study or learning skills, for example, translation, deduction, working on keywords, using available resources, mnemonics, taking notes.

The prefix 'meta' literally means 'beyond'. Metacognition therefore means 'beyond cognition'. O'Malley and Chamot (1990) use the cognition/metacognition distinction extensively in their own construction of learning strategy taxonomies. For them, a metacognitive strategy involves thinking about language or the learning process. Such a strategy acts less on language itself than knowledge about processing language. Preplanning a linguistic task, monitoring while it is being carried out, and evaluation after it has been completed would all be considered metacognitive strategies.

Besides these examples, O'Malley and Chamot list many other strategies, a good deal of which are identical or very similar to ones we have already referred to. For example, for O'Malley and Chamot, metacognitive strategies also include 'rehearsal' of linguistic components, selective attention in reading and listening, and developing an understanding of the conditions which facilitate personal learning.

To these two basic categories of learning strategies, O'Malley and Chamot add a third: social strategies. This grouping is used to refer to the strategies involved in social contexts – for example, cooperation or asking for clarification – or control over the emotion and affection necessarily implicated in learning a foreign language.

We offer these three categories of strategy not as another attempt to provide a satisfactory taxonomy for guiding research, but as a classificatory scheme which highlights a particular underlying learning theory. We can now make a distinction between linguistic knowledge – competence – and the mental processes involved in acquiring it – metacognitive, cognitive and social strategies. Our earlier discussion of declarative and procedural knowledge is relevant in that each of these 'orders of knowledge' can be expressed in their terms. In other words, it may be that learners are automatically using the sort of metacognitive, cognitive and social strategies listed. If this is the case, they are already proceduralised; perhaps to the extent that they are not aware of what they are doing. On the other hand, learning strategies can be 'declared' so as to be available to the learner in an explicit manner, who may then choose to adopt them (or not). It may be that, much as in the case of linguistic knowledge discussed above, different strategies are used in different contexts according to particular linguistic and learning demands, and in a conscious or unconscious manner. We will explore these themes further in Chapters 3 and 5 when we look at the strategy use of particular learners.

Clearly, both in the application of cognitive theory to language competence and learning strategies, some sort of development gradient is implied. Just as some parts of language are easier to learn than others, so some strategies are easier to use than others. For example, use of dictionaries to provide a translation of a word is relatively low level and unsophisticated when compared to the complex usage of inference and deduction to ascertain meaning. This point may also imply that easier strategies are acquired by early learners, the more difficult ones come later (see Chesterfield and Chesterfield 1985). Similarly, returning to our discussion of the 'good language learner', it is unsurprising to find that a successful learner is a frequent user of a wide range of strategies; the opposite also being true (see O'Malley and Chamot 1990). Furthermore, they also adopt a multi-purpose approach, using strategies in combination rather than isolation (see Graham 1997). The vertical axis of Figure 2.1 on page 45 allows us to capture this difference between the successful and poor learner. The successful language learner attacks the task using both ends of the axis bottom-up and top-down; the less successful learner may operate only at the level of word-for-word translation. A poor learner uses few strategies. Table 2.1 is an attempt to express these dichotomies. It is a conceptual scheme produced in the light of engaging with data from empirical research. It seeks to demonstrate the issues at stake in the success, stage, range and type and frequency of strategy use by learners in their developing linguistic competence.

We have taken time to set out these conceptual ideas in order to provide a theoretical basis for the rest of the book. We do not want to be overly abstract and obscure. However, we want to go beyond a simple assertion of the importance of learning strategies and the description of another taxonomy more pertinent to our own particular context. We have set out continua of declarative and procedural knowledge, metacognitive and cognitive strategies, and knowledge of and about language in general terms. However, we do not want to lose

Table 2.1 Continua in strategy use

Easy	Hard
Acquired early	Acquired later
Low attainers	High attainers
↓	↓
Less frequent use	More frequent use
Narrow range	Wider range
Less helpful strategies	More helpful strategies
Bottom-up	Bottom-up and top-down
Word for word	Meaning
Translation	Inferencing
Repetition	Applying rules
Formulaic phrases	Monitoring production

sight of the learner. In 1989 Skehan wrote of the tendency of linguistic research to deal with generalities rather than individual differences, while it is the latter which should perhaps be of more concern, since it is as particular learners, not as groups, that competence is developed. Among such differences as aptitude, attitude and motivation Skehan also refers to strategies. Indeed, we would expect that every learner, and for every developmental stage of their learning, has a particular strategy profile. Strategies which are employed to cope with the early stages of language learning and then proceduralised as linguistic demands increase, are complemented by further strategies to facilitate the new level of competence. Similarly, some strategies are conducive to particular learner types and not others. Wesche (1981) has shown how matching method to learner type may facilitate rate of learning; in this case, grammar–analytical methods with deductive reasoners, and communicative language teaching with more socially affective types. There is no reason not to believe that strategies are affected in the same way. So social, inferencing strategies will be best employed by learners whose preference is for inductive methods and in contexts where there is high contact with native speakers of the language. More academic, deductive strategies will be used by those favouring an analytical approach to knowing a language. Skehan also refers to the work of Witkin (1962, 1979), who has devised tests to reflect the way individuals perceive and organise the world. 'Field-dependent' people see the world as an unanalysed whole and do not attend to particular elements. These types are socially orientated and sensitive to others. 'Field-independent' individuals, on the other hand, are more detached and impersonal, and able to view particulars in the field independently from the whole. The extrapolation of these types to the case of language learning is to see field-dependent individuals as again more attuned to the totality of language experience rather than the constituent parts of language; and the reverse for the field-independent people. Cognitive style may then deeply affect which strategies are used, and which are used most successfully. Cultural background may also be a significant factor in determining how learners approach a task as, for example, one study comparing Nigerian and Japanese learners suggests (see Parry 1993).

To these individual differences we would add differences of age and gender (see Politzer 1983, Bügel and Buunk 1996 and Bacon 1992). The particular context for this book is secondary school pupils (aged 11–18). These are formative years and we know that cognitive, as well as affective and behavioural, maturity has an enormous impact on learning. We also know that in each of these there are important differences between boys and girls. In the next chapter, we look at some of these individual differences in strategy use in detail based on research of particular learners: two girls and a boy across the secondary school age range. We then go on to consider ways of helping learners to use strategies more and what happened with a group of teachers when they did. By way of introduction to these topics, we wish to conclude the present chapter with a return to the pedagogic implications of our discussion so far.

What it is to teach

Chapter 1 of this book looked at the search for a language-teaching methodology, and Chapter 2 then considered the type of learning theory which might be justified. Cognitive theory supplied us with an explanatory scheme, which allowed us to connect different orders of knowledge – from the deeply inner psychological to the most outer social and cultural – in a way which highlighted the actual experience of language learning. We examined what the good language learner does and considered the possible strategies they use. In this discussion we made the point that one of the attractions of this area of applied linguistic research for teachers (and in this case it might be unique) is the pedagogic implications it has. In other words, there is the obvious inference that if we can understand better the learning process, then we can construct pedagogic conditions to facilitate it. As one part of this, we can catalogue the strategies used by learners at various developmental stages and in particular contexts, so that we can then teach others what to do in order to facilitate their learning. At this point, it is probably worth returning to issues of curricula – how strategies might feature in them – as a way of indicating how we might shape learning from a strategy point of view.

We can see how, as part of the National Curriculum in Modern Foreign Languages in England, pupils are required to cover a range of skills and understanding. These are directly related to learning strategies:

Language skills

Pupils should be taught to:

(a) listen attentively and listen for gist and detail;

(b) follow instructions and directions;
(c) ask about meanings, seek clarification or repetition;
(d) ask and answer questions, and give instructions;
(e) ask for and give information and explanations;
(f) imitate pronunciation and intonation patterns;
(g) initiate and develop conversations;
(h) express agreement, disagreement, personal feelings and opinions;
(i) describe and discuss present, past and future events;
(j) skim and scan texts, including databases where appropriate, for information;
(k) copy words, phrases and sentences;
(l) make notes from what they hear or read;
(m) summarise and report the main points of spoken or written texts;
(n) redraft their writing to improve its accuracy and presentation, e.g. by word-processing;
(o) vary language to suit context, audience and purpose.

Language-learning skills and knowledge of language

Pupils should be taught to:

(a) learn by heart phrases and short extracts, e.g. rhymes, poems, songs, jokes, tongue twisters;
(b) acquire strategies for committing familiar language to memory;
(c) develop their independence in language learning and use;
(d) use dictionaries and reference materials;
(e) use context and other clues to interpret meaning;
(f) understand and apply patterns, rules and exceptions in language forms and structures;
(g) use their knowledge to experiment with language;
(h) understand and use formal and informal language;
(i) develop strategies for dealing with the unpredictable.

(DFE 1995: p. 3)

Many of the above link directly to the sorts of strategies discussed elsewhere in this chapter. There is certainly an attempt here to go beyond a simple list of grammar points or communicative contexts. For example, there is a whole set of social and metacognitive strategies embedded in this list. Other curricula are now beginning to include these dimensions in their framework when drawing up the content for language learning and teaching.

The Common European Framework – *Modern Languages: Learning, Teaching and Assessment*, published by the Council of Europe (1996) – similarly attempts to provide greater sophistication in conceptualising language learning and consequent teaching. Here, learners' competencies are listed as *general competencies* and *communicative language competencies*. The former are proposed in terms of 'Declarative Knowledge'(referred to as *savoir*), 'Existential Knowledge' (*savoir-être*) and the 'Ability to Learn' (*savoir-apprendre*) (ibid., pp. 39–57). The latter refer to the familiar list of linguistic, sociolinguistic and pragmatic features. However, all these are followed by an extensive list of strategies, categorised under reception, production, interaction and mediation. The whole accent is on a shift away from teaching method to learner knowledge:

> Learners may (be expected/required to) develop their study and heuristic skills and their acceptance for their own learning:
> (a) simply as 'spin-off' from language learning and teaching, without any special planning or provision;
> (b) by progressively transferring responsibility for learning from the teacher to the pupils/students and encouraging them to reflect on their learning and to share this experience with other learners;
> (c) by systematically raising the learners' awareness of the learning/teaching processes in which they are participating;
> (d) by engaging learners as participants in experimentation with different methodological options;
> (e) by getting learners to recognise their own cognitive style and to develop their learning strategies accordingly.
>
> (ibid., p. 94)

This emphasis on 'learning to learn' marks an intention to approach language learning from a different direction: rather than a perfect method, it focuses on the learner – their particular competence profile, learning styles and developmental stage. In emphasising this objective, the theoretical framework we have outlined above is particularly pertinent as it indicates the processes which may be brought into play in pedagogic contexts. It requires us to think in terms of knowledge *about* language as well as knowledge *of* language, and to include tasks and activities to develop both. It calls for a serious consideration of the autonomous learner, and what this means for the autonomy of the teacher. The role of the teacher changes from teaching the language to teaching the students to learn. The learner develops the skills and strategies to develop their own communicative competence in the range of features highlighted in Chapter 1. It creates a 'linguistic individual' who is not distinct from the character and personality of the learner. The two are not divorced: rather, one is an expression of the other. The question then is how to do it?

There is little reason to suppose that listing strategies and then teaching them to learners will be more successful than listing grammar and teaching it to learners. We know now that the link between knowing and using is not linear. What is needed is to tackle the question of how to organise teaching in order to facilitate this 'learning to learn'. Some strategies might indeed be taught effectively in an explicit manner. Others may best be 'induced' in the course of involvement with particular activities and tasks. In these cases, the pedagogic objective is not the conventional one of a particular linguistic point – vocabulary, grammar, comprehension – but the development of particular strategies.

The advantage that the latter has over the former is that rather than being another grain of salt to shoulder in the hope that it will be recalled when required, it develops particular relationships to language and the processes of learning that language and has much greater applications: both in actual language use and the pedagogic activity involved in developing a personal linguistic competence.

Part Two of this book explores the whole question of strategy training. However, we conclude Part One with three case examples of learners and the strategies they use. We include them to give some illustrative and practical weight to the conceptual discussion so far and as a reminder of the particular messiness of the real world compared with the relative neatness of learning and teaching in theory. However, we would not want these to be seen as worlds apart. Rather, we hope that the two parts of this work will be read symbiotically.

3   Learners' strategies

Introduction

This chapter looks in detail at the language-learning strategies of three
adolescent learners. The three vary from beginner to intermediate levels (ages
12, 15 and 17 years). How does their use of strategies connect to the findings
discussed in Chapter 2? Are they typical 'good language learners'? Does the stage
they have reached in their language learning map itself neatly against a background continuum from the use of 'basic' to more complex strategies? Do their
cognitive styles and the nature of the task also affect their strategy use? These
are the questions this chapter seeks to address in order to show up the reality of
students learning language.

The information offered here comes from an investigation into the strategy use
of particular learners. As previously noted, much of the research and literature on
learning strategies is concerned with bilingual learners and with adults. English is
the language being learned in the majority of cases. The case examples offered
here are different in both respects: the individuals involved are learning French
within the British school system; and they are adolescent.

In order to offer a degree of cross-case comparison, we have structured our
discussion of each of the cases under a series of common headings:

- What does the learner like and dislike in their language learning?
- How do they set about their learning?
- How do they operate in speaking and reading?
- Summarising comments

We also add some more speculative comments concerning which further
strategies would help each learner. Finally, we conclude with some discussion
which compares one learner with another and raises issues of individual strategy
use and developmental stage.

Collecting information on strategy use

The following case examples are based on two particular skill areas: one
productive, speaking; and the other receptive, reading. These skills were selected

in order to offer a range of strategies, but without going into extensive detail of every aspect of an individual's language learning. One way of trying to elucidate what learners think about their learning is to use 'think aloud' and retrospective techniques (see Faerch and Kasper 1987). Here, learners are either asked to provide an oral commentary while they undertake a task in the target language, or to reflect retrospectively after carrying it out. The reading task for the eldest of the three learners was an extract from a French novel taken from a current coursebook aimed at her age group. The tasks for the other two learners were books from a published reading scheme, resembling strip cartoons in that they contain a series of pictures. Each of the three learners was asked to read through their text and to think aloud any thoughts they had while making sense of it. These episodes were recorded. For the speaking task, the conversation was semi-structured in that specific stages in discussion were envisaged and topic areas planned to elicit particular types of language, most notably tenses, prompted by a series of photos of the learner's family, past holidays and previous home. Towards the end of the session, the learners answered some general questions in French about their family and their school and then were invited to question the interlocutor on any topics of their choice. The conversations were recorded and played back to the subjects who paused the tape recorder to comment on performance, feelings and thinking at the time or in retrospect. These comments were also recorded. At the end of the session, the learners were asked general questions in English such as whether they enjoyed French, found any particular skills easy or hard and how they approached their homework. The recordings from all tasks were transcribed.

Such retrospection is an opportunity of accessing what is in the learner's mind immediately after an encounter with a second-language learning task in a way which connects closely with the authenticity of experience in carrying it out. As time passes, learners forget what they did, what they were thinking, and interpret their reactions to the task from memory which distorts what actually occurred. Immediate retrospection attempts to avoid such distortion by probing the learners' thinking while thoughts are still running through their minds. Nevertheless, there are evident limitations to the technique. It is difficult to select a reading text that is sufficiently accessible but also offers opportunities for learners to deploy the full range of strategies they have at their disposal. Our case-example learners mostly operate in a school context rather than an 'acquisition-rich environment'. This means that the strategies developed tend to emphasise the pedagogic rather than the natural, social strategies which may arise in interactions with native speakers of the language. Such a background automatically precludes the use of some strategies and renders problematic comparison with some of the studies described in Chapter 2. There is also a tension between what remains implicit and what can be made explicit. If the learner does not choose to comment on something, this does not necessarily mean that they are not using it. Indeed, we might surmise that one becomes less conscious of what one is doing as proficiency is gained in a particular strategy. The problems of 'think aloud' procedures in the reading task are evident in the eldest learner's comment that: 'it's like in an interview when someone asks you a hard question and you want to think about it but then you think you don't want the silence there, so you talk and so you can't think and it's a vicious circle'. Each of the learners commented on the artificiality of the speaking task and, in some cases, they found difficulty even in recalling the events shown in the photos. Their different preferences for either answering the interlocutor's general questions or discussing the photos do appear to reflect differences in cognitive styles. For this reason they are discussed towards the end of the chapter, after a picture of each learner has been presented.

As noted earlier in this book, it is not easy to get inside the 'black box' of the human brain and find out what is going on there. We work with what we can get, which, despite the limitations, provides food for thought and connects with the issues raised in the last chapter. The following accounts are based on what each of the learners were able to tell us about their language learning: interviews were transcribed and analysed according to the issues raised in the good language learner research. Their own retrospective comments were also transcribed and matched against the emerging picture of their learning styles and processes. Finally, linguistic analyses were made of their actual utterances in French in order to catalogue what language they were using and other structural features of their use of the foreign language.

Our three learners are Sophie, Jenny and Ben. We make our comments in the light of discussion and comparison with the learning-strategy literature. A fuller account of the data analysis can be found in Grenfell and Harris 1995, where detailed linguistic description is given. In the present context, we offer our case examples as illustrative accounts. In many places, we quote verbatim from transcripts of our discussions with them. In other places, and in order to provide readable narrative and cover as many features of their learning as possible, we offer our summary comments and interpretations based on discussion with them and analysis of their linguistic utterances. We move from the eldest and most advanced of the three to the youngest learner. We therefore begin with the eldest learner, Sophie, then consider Jenny and finally Ben, the youngest.

Sophie

Sophie is an 'advanced' language learner in that she is currently studying for an Advanced Level Examination in French in England. This means that she is in her seventh year of language learning; although, as a limited number of hours each week are devoted to language studies, we might consider her learning as being part-time. The qualification enables her to undertake undergraduate studies. Her actual level of linguistic competence might then possibly be best described as 'advanced–intermediate'.

Sophie likes French but does not find it easy. She is sociable and communicative, and yet seemingly has chronic problems with accuracy. Sometimes, what she knows about the language just does not seem to connect with what she produces, and she gets frustrated with her own mistakes. She is well motivated and has had regular contact with France. However, this was some years ago and she has only been to France sporadically since then. Nevertheless, she likes France and the French way of life.

What does Sophie like in her language learning? And what does she not like?

Learning vocabulary is a plus: 'putting words into a sentence and learning phrases are what I like. You can just slam some things in and you know they're (i.e. the teachers) going to go: "oh what a beautiful phrase"'. She is good at English too and enjoys style over accuracy. This comes through in her writing. She knows that written French does not have to be complicated. The writer has the choice of what to say and how to say it. This puts her in control of the language and how to use it. She hates prose translations, especially those from English into French, because 'none of it is your choice'. Listening is hard too for a similar reason; although it does not require the accuracy needed in transferring from one to another language and is therefore easier than translation.

This juxtaposition of accuracy and control is evident in her attitude to grammar and vocabulary when speaking: 'I find grammar comes naturally if I can talk naturally and it doesn't come naturally at all if I am translating from English into French; like when I am relaxed, I have the space to stick in a subjunctive or a conditional'. For this learner, command of vocabulary is closely connected with the degree to which this mental space is available and her ability to work on her accuracy: 'when you're not searching for words then you can keep an eye on your grammar'. We will explore what this 'keeping an eye on grammar' looks like when we discuss the speaking task in more detail.

How does she set about her learning?

Sophie reports that learning vocabulary is important to her and she tackles this task by using a number of different strategies. She says she writes words out, identifies items as important by highlighting in colour and places new words in sentences and recites them out loud. She also describes how she uses mental tests between English to French and French to English.

She states that grammar is more difficult to remember. Grammar rules are copied out. She understands these at the time but does not bring them to her practice later. It is as if the two systems are separate; each not communicating with the other. Still, she makes up some of her own rules to check her practice. For example, in remembering whether to use 'à' or 'en' before a town or country, she thinks of the 'small à connecting with the smaller town'. She also spots symmetries between English and French: for example, 'mal à l'aise' connects almost perfectly with the English 'ill at ease'.

She is hard-working and conscientious. Homework is always done. Sophie's enjoyment of literature probably explains why she seems to have a more systematic system for revising it than revising the language itself: 'I'll reread the books, make notes and read through past essays'. In terms of directly learning the language, she confesses that: 'I do my homework but I don't really do independent stuff enough'. She has been encouraged by her teacher to read authentic French magazines and listen to the radio, but rarely does so.

How does Sophie operate in speaking and reading?

Sophie describes how speaking is an opportunity to be herself, to take control of her own language. Increased autonomy leads to increased control, which leads to increased confidence and increased accuracy. This means that asking questions in a conversation is easier than answering them, as in the former she has more influence on what topics are dealt with (the ones she finds most familiar and is most comfortable talking about) and on the progress of conversation. The more she feels in control of the conversation, the more she can keep an eye on her grammar. What does this 'keeping an eye on grammar' look like in practice? Monitoring clearly goes on, but takes various forms. For example, Sophie is keen to operate the grammar rule which makes verbs negative – 'je ne les ai pas vus' – and understands that 'pas' can be replaced with a whole lot of other indefinite pronouns: rien, personne, que, jamais. However, in the past she has forgotten to miss out the 'pas' with these. She tells herself to do this but then over-compensates and omits the 'pas' as well in straight negatives.

She is clearly comfortable to correct initial utterances; sometimes visual representations seem to facilitate her perception of errors. For example, when trying to say that Shakespeare's comedies are not as deep as his tragedies she corrects 'n'ont pas' (haven't) to 'ne sont pas' (aren't) because 'it didn't make sense . . . I have a mental image of having something and someone holding something and that just didn't go'. Similarly, she corrects 'son pommes' to 'ses pommes': 'I know that 'son' is for one apple and 'ses' is for three'. Sometimes, correction is intuitive: at one point 'notre' is corrected to the plural 'nos' preceding 'vacances': 'I didn't think about it at all'. Monitoring of this sort is fast and instant. However, it does not always work. When looking at photos of herself as a child, she said 'nous sommes enfants' instead of using the imperfect. The moment passes, and it is only on playback that she notices the error. Monitoring and recall can bring on a crisis: the mind goes blank, so that even what is easily known cannot be remembered. At one point in the conversation she wants to say 'I cannot remember'. 'Souvenir' is spotted in advance as a complicated verb to use. It seems as if she is in a panic trying to remember how to employ it. The relatively simple verb for 'can' is then also lost as she loses control over her linguistic competence. It is a sort of 'mental paralysis'.

'Fillers' are an asset. 'Alors', 'Bof' are used – 'they give you time to think'. Variety in the use of these is at a premium: 'bien sûr' and 'puis' are also employed extensively – 'I stick them in just because I like the sound of them'. Having a stock of these 'fillers' is a major component in constructing authentic-sounding dialogue: 'people pause naturally in conversation and so there is no reason not to pause in a French way'. We will later see that Ben (our youngest learner) shares this concern to replicate a 'natural' conversation, although lacks the use of 'fillers' to buy himself thinking time.

The same points might be made about 'pre-packaged forms', such as: 'c'était bien/c'était vraiment bien/c'était merveilleuse'. These forms also buy her time and lend an air of authenticity to her language. Some of these are instantly gained from the individual with whom Sophie is speaking. The interlocutor offers: 'une sorte de bateau, non?' as a form of circumlocution for an aquaflume and she immediately replies: 'une sorte de bateau, oui, oui'. She is sometimes able not only to repeat the words but to reapply them subsequently in a different context. Thus, at an early stage in the conversation, the interlocutor supplied the words 'caractère' and 'identité' to support her attempts to describe her cousins. At a later stage, she uses the same terms to describe the houses in the street in which she used to live: 'ils ont beaucoup de caractère, beaucoup d'identité'.

In reading a passage, her comments show how she goes for general meaning before the detail of individual words and syntax. She skips non-essential words, and starts by skimming to spot what she already recognises. She then cuts up the passage into recognisable boundaries and deals with each one in turn, looking 'at the chunks of things that mean things together'. Specifics are related to her growing hypothesis around what the text is about. Boundaries between 'chunks' of language are then used as guiding meaning against which specifics of vocabulary and grammar are checked. Where there are problems, inferences and guessing are used by setting the global understanding against the detail of individual words. This approach is akin to what we described as *top-down* and *bottom-up* – from general meaning to individual word level – in Chapter 2; working from the latter to the former. This multi-pronged approach is successful when confirmation is received about meaning. The problems start for her when this is not so, and, in some cases, the whole global meaning of the text is challenged by a detail which, seemingly, does not fit: 'sometimes most of it will be fine and straightforward, but then there will be some things that I just can't do'. It seems to be swings and roundabouts. Linguistic competence works on meaning until it does not. At this point, mental paralysis seems to set in; all there is to do is translate word for word into English, which even then might not make sense of the language.

Summarising comments

What we describe confirms that Sophie seems to be at a middle stage in her linguistic development and has a developed though limited range of learning strategies at her disposal: she can monitor effectively and has a range of inferencing strategies which serve her well. She also makes use of an established list of 'fillers' and pre-packaged forms. However, there are gaps in her knowledge. When she falls into one of these, she guesses wildly or panics.

Her style of learning matches the characteristics of the global/field-dependent learner who prefers social interaction to analytical analysis and application of formal rules. For example, she finds it hard to discipline herself to remember the gender with vocabulary. Interestingly, she interprets this as a sign of laziness rather than a cognitive preference: 'it's in my nature to be lazy; I know I should sort out my gender thing'. The detail does not concern her. What matters is the nature of the social interaction: sometimes, the struggle to say exactly what she intends obscures the possibilities of rewording something or saying an innocent mistruth which has little consequence in the conversation but would buy her important management control. She is struggling to be herself in the language, but this is constantly being disrupted. Such disruption also undermines the very processes which may possibly be at her disposal in order to construct this 'other' in the foreign language. However, this openness also has advantages; for example, it allows her to navigate intuitively through meaning and linguistic relations with others.

What are the most useful strategies that would allow Sophie to maximise her potential?

It seems that Sophie has already acquired a range of useful on-the-spot strategies for conveying and understanding meanings. She needs now to stand back from her concern to assert her identity and become more focused both about her learning and about her language use. She could develop a greater range of communication strategies, particularly 'message adjustment' and 'circumlocution' to avoid the mental panic induced when she anticipates a problem like the manipulation of a complex verb. To tackle the frustration she feels at making avoidable mistakes, she might benefit from adopting a less mechanical approach to learning grammar rules than simply copying them out when: 'it goes in at the time but I don't seem to remember it'. She could, for example, capitalise on her strong visual learning style; an account of the use of colour-coding to remember gender for example is provided in Chapter 5. She could also exploit her intuitive 'feel' ('it just sounds right') by saying sentences exemplifying particular grammar points out loud. Although she is prepared to 'play with' the language orally, she does not transfer the same risk-taking to learning grammar rules, by generating her own written examples, once she has understood the rule. In contrast to Jenny, as we shall see, Sophie does not attempt to deduce common patterns to help her recall the rules. Finally, when she reads, she could try to spot the application of particular rules, for example, tenses and check whether she understands why they are appropriate in that context. These strategies that focus on grammatical awareness might also help her break down some of the pre-packaged forms on which she still relies.

Our next example is at a less advanced level and shows a different range of strategies.

Jenny

Jenny is 15 years old, in her fifth year of language learning and is studying for her GCSE examinations. These are public examinations taken in England, Wales and Northern Ireland at the end of compulsory schooling (age 16 years). High-attaining pupils are usually entered for the GCSE examination in each of the eight or nine subjects they are studying. Less successful pupils may be entered for fewer subjects. Jenny, an able pupil, is entered for nine subjects, including French, where her teachers expect her to do well. A high grade in the examination would allow her to study French for the Advanced Level examination. Her level of linguistic competence might be best described as 'intermediate'.

She enjoys French, particularly following her recent exchange trip to France: 'it was brilliant . . . I was just a lot more confident . . . I might get the thing wrong but that didn't matter because it was just about communication and if she understood what I was getting at . . . you've got to get a message across so . . . you've just got to try everything'. From her speaking and reading tasks, it seems that it is only in such authentic contexts that she feels free to abandon her otherwise predominant concern for grammatical accuracy.

What does Jenny like and dislike in her language learning?

The concern to 'get it right' means that Jenny prefers writing to the pressures of 'on-line processing' involved in speaking: 'if I've got time to work things out, like when I'm writing, then I can work it out but if I've got to get it on the spur of the moment, then I might not get it . . .'. Reading too removes the pressure to produce a perfect performance. Indeed, the written word appears to play a more important part in Jenny's language monitoring than with Sophie, who uses image associations. Jenny: 'it's a lot harder when you're saying it straight off to think of how it would look . . . you try and visualise how it would look when it was written down . . . that's what I do when I'm speaking'. She thus finds the use of the conditional tense hard: 'because they all sound the same at the end . . . I know the difference when I write them'. Her trip to France provided her with some tangible connections between grammar and meaning but through social impact rather than image representations. She remembers the masculine and feminine forms of 'cousin/cousine' because a girl at the French school was offended that she addressed her as 'Martin' (the masculine form of the first name), instead of 'Martine' (the feminine form).

How does Jenny set about her learning?

Jenny takes her schoolwork seriously and has reflected on her own learning patterns: 'I think it helps to revise with a friend 'cos like otherwise it's really hard to sit back and learn the vocab. and French is one of the worst subjects for getting side-tracked'. She has begun to internalise French-spelling conventions: 'in the first year I used to have to sit there and learn each different word . . . but now the minute I see what the word looks like I, I can sort of learn it in my head. I suppose it's like when you're little and you're learning to spell English words . . . like you look at a word now and you're bound to be able to spell it OK in a shorter amount of time'. Much of her time is devoted to learning grammar rules: 'I go over the grammar as well so I know all the grammar rules, adjective endings'. Jenny has a more active approach to memorising rules than Sophie who just copies them out, since for the last few years, Jenny has been independently noting down key verbs at the back of her book: 'Some of them have got patterns and I try to work out which ones are connected and then that's what helps you to remember'.

How does Jenny operate in speaking and reading?

Jenny does not find it easy to communicate in the artificial context of the speaking task. Her anxiety is reflected in the short utterances she produces and she needs constant prompting to elaborate on the photos. Unlike Sophie, she rarely makes a mistake in gender as long as she uses familiar expressions ('mon frère, à la maison de ma tante, à côté de la voiture, mon père'). The meaning of the word and its gender appear to be stored in her memory alongside each other. Longer utterances are restricted to those occasions when she can produce an answer on topics already well rehearsed in school or can take control by asking familiar questions. They too are error free: 'elle s'appelle Jane, je suis alleé en Grèce, on a visité les villes, il y a du soleil, vous habitez où, vous aimez le village?' She is able to monitor some simple phrases in advance, explaining of 'elle était difficile', 'so I was putting it in the past', and of 'mon cousin', 'I was trying to get Matthew right because he's like not feminine is he?' Faced with less predictable questions, she seems reluctant to risk using *pre-packaged forms* to generate new meanings. When she does try, she appears to experience the same kind of mental paralysis as Sophie. It seems that suddenly the whole system breaks down, with basic errors such as omission of verbs, prepositions or even articles: 'c'est un, une vacance camping en France', 'moi et Ben mmm', 'er mmm ville de Pays de Galles . . . c'est mmm', 'mmm pense mm le Noël avec ma amie'. She rarely attempts to correct these utterances; it seems that she has to be right first time either by using a pre-packaged form or by having sufficient time to monitor in advance. When she can do neither, the mental panic induced means that she lacks the confidence to apply the rules she knows and to monitor retrospectively.

In comparison, Sophie is more willing to launch into communication and more comfortable with correcting her initial attempts. Sophie does however have a wider range of 'fillers' to give herself time to think than Jenny, whose use of 'fillers' is restricted to 'je pense' or 'très' to respond to the interlocutor's utterances: 'Il faisait chaud? Oui, très chaud', 'C'était joli? Oui, très joli'. Jenny's failure to use 'fillers' may stem simply from a limited linguistic repertoire but it may also reflect her perception that the speaking task bears no resemblance to authentic communication, where, as Sophie noted, hesitations and re-phrasings are natural. It is noticeable that while Jenny's use of language may appear limited, she has little difficulty in understanding the interlocutor, who does not need to adjust the speed of his delivery.

Jenny appears to tackle the reading task with greater confidence than the speaking task. Like Sophie, her approach is top-down to bottom-up and she is prepared to skip non-essential words: 'so even though I didn't know what the individual words meant I know exactly what they were saying . . . the sense of it'. The text she reads offers more support than Sophie's and she makes extensive use of the pictures to reach an initial hypothesis of what it is about. Where she knows sufficient numbers of words, or can guess them because they are cognates, she uses inferencing effectively to fill in the missing elements: 'My domestiques? Something to do with domestic, mmm I see, my servant-type people lived in another little house . . . au fond du jardin . . . I don't know what that means . . . but it's probably something like in the bottom of the garden'. She appears to tolerate the uncertainty of 'not knowing' and to have the confidence to find ways round it more readily in the reading task than in the speaking task. She is more prepared to remedy false starts, monitoring for meaning effectively. She explains: 'But then I thought door to my garden, that's not right . . . you don't have a door to the garden, so I realised it must be gate'. Reading allows her time to bring her grammatical knowledge to bear and she initially tackles a difficult sentence confidently: 'That's about himself . . . 'cos it's *je me suis* and that's not a bank 'cos that's masculine'. Where she then discovers that the sentence contains too many unfamiliar words to permit any kind of global understanding, such analysis may not even then reveal the sense of the language: 'I don't know what that word is and I don't know what that word is, so I can't . . .' Unless a certain number of words are already known or can be guessed by Jenny, grammatical analysis alone cannot compensate.

At times, understanding a sufficient amount of a sentence appears to trigger off recall of a previously learned but forgotten word, perhaps by narrowing down the field of possible meanings to be searched through. She struggles with the word 'meubles' (furniture) at the beginning of the text. When she encounters it again later in the passage and has established the overall context: 'I heard . . . is it something confusing . . . inside the house. It was like as if someone was moving . . . the furniture ah I remember now . . . I'd forgotten that word furniture . . . I've just remembered'. A sort of *semantic mapping* may occur, some words being associated according to the particular topic groups covered in school, even when the context is quite different. Thus she recognises 'faible' for *weak* moon: 'I remember learning *faible* when it was "I've got a weak heart" when we did the doctors and things . . . so you remember words in bits and that's how I knew that'.

Summarising comments

The picture gained is of a learner, who, though at the intermediate stage in her linguistic development, operates very differently according to the task she is tackling. Jenny: in school 'You do things like put your hand up . . . we don't actually do speaking very much, that's one of the least things we do' and: 'Sometimes I know how to spell a word but I don't know how to say it'. The type of teaching she is exposed to therefore appears not to conform to even the limited interpretation of communicative language teaching outlined in Chapter 1. On the other hand, her own style of learning seems to represent the field-independent learner, who enjoys analytical analysis and deducing and applying formal rules. Hence, speaking, as the fastest skill, is hardest for Jenny. Her cognitive preference for the written word is evident both in the way she visualises words, while she is speaking, and in the ease with which she can absorb spellings just by looking at the word, suggesting she may have a photographic memory. The demands of genuine exchanges with native speakers may serve to bypass the dependence on the written word, but otherwise Jenny finds it hard to express her identity and becomes so preoccupied with presenting an image of herself as an accurate speaker of the language that she is almost tongue-tied and fails to draw on her underlying linguistic knowledge. Whereas Sophie is happy to 'play with' the language, Jenny's approach is to 'play safe'. In contrast, the reading task suggests a good language learner who, in spite of the fact that she has a more limited vocabulary than Sophie, has advanced inferencing strategies, monitors for meaning effectively and is ready to constantly modify her original hypotheses on the basis of new information.

What are the most useful strategies that would allow Jenny to maximise her potential?

It would appear that Jenny has already developed useful strategies for reading and writing. Although listening places more demands on her, since she cannot rely on the written word, her range of vocabulary and knowledge of formal rules allows her to cope. It also allows her to communicate orally in situations where her concern about grammatical accuracy is overridden by the need to convey meaning to those who cannot speak English. Problems arise when there is no genuinely communicative context. While the 'self-talk strategy' (developing a dialogue with oneself) identified by O'Malley and Chamot (1990) may help to reduce her anxiety about presenting a perfect performance, it may be difficult to change her fundamental learning style. The strategies that would seem most useful are those that foster her confidence by buying her time to monitor in advance. These will be discussed in greater detail in Part Two alongside suggestions for how to teach them, but they include:

- turn-giving gambits: 'what do you think? I'd like to know your opinion on . . . I see what you mean, that's interesting, I hadn't thought of that';
- topic manipulation and turn-getting gambits to move the conversation into familiar areas: 'talking of; incidentally; personally I think that X is more important';
- avoidance strategies: 'it all depends what you mean by . . .; it's difficult to say';
- fillers: 'well; that's true; gosh';
- all-purpose words: 'thingamabob'.

This latter strategy along with circumlocution might reduce the panic she feels when she predicts that she will need a word that she does not know. Where these strategies cannot be put into operation fast enough to keep up with the flow of conversation, some reassurance that it is perfectly acceptable to correct an initial utterance might be useful along with the means to do it in French: 'I meant . . .; I made a mistake there'. Above all, she needs convincing that she should say as much as she can and that 'getting it in' (whether a verb or a noun) is more important than 'getting it right' in terms of the appropriate tense marker or gender.

Finally, Jenny needs to develop the means to exploit the presence of the interlocutor, not only by turn-giving gambits but also by listening carefully to what she or he says and using the language for oneself, as Sophie did. It is noticeable that she is unwilling to use the strategy of *questioning for clarification*: 'How do you say . . .?' Understandably perhaps, given the context of the GCSE examination, the picture she appears to have is of a presentation to a critical audience, rather than a shared negotiation of meanings. Whereas it may be difficult to persuade her otherwise, the development of communication strategies might provide one concrete means of feeling more in control of the situation.

Ben

Ben is 12 years old and has been studying French for a year and a half. His level of linguistic competence might then be described as that of the 'beginner'. He is less motivated to learn French than Jenny. His holidays to France took place before he started to learn it and: 'On campsites everybody was English so I didn't really hear much French'. Although he believes French is more useful, he finds Welsh easier, as he has been learning it since he was 7 years old. Nevertheless, he is quite confident, as the teacher has put him in the 'top class'. His perception of language seems to be that it consists of vocabulary and set phrases and he is uncertain what grammar is.

What does Ben like and dislike in his language learning?

Ben appears to accept the routines of language learning that he is offered. He assumes that each topic will entail learning vocabulary and writing conversations. He enjoys using the language creatively: 'Like, we'll choose a famous person and we'll, like, do a TV report and ask some questions that we've learned'. He perceives the goal of language learning not just as communication but also as an expression of identity. This may also be a factor in determining his preference for Welsh, since he now can confidently engage in quite lengthy dialogues, such as negotiating an outing. In French, however: 'I seem, like, to be equivalent to a 2-year-old . . . I just know I maybe sound stupid in France because it'd be so basic to them, when in school all the teachers are going "oh that's brilliant"'. He does not perceive accuracy as an issue in how his identity is perceived. For him the struggle is to find the words he needs to make sense.

How does Ben set about his learning?

Ben uses the strategy of 'look–cover–test–check' to learn lists of vocabulary. When he has to learn phrases, he repeats them aloud or reads them over and over again. He does not try to generate similar sentences for himself. He is aware of different attitudes to learning within his class and different levels of ability: 'I think the girls probably try harder but a lot of the boys just have a natural ability in doing things. The girls seem to revise and get the same grades as the boys who haven't revised. Also it can be different – some boys revise a lot and they get the same as the other boys that don't revise – it just depends on who you are really'. He considers that he works hard.

How does Ben operate in speaking and reading?

Unlike Sophie and Jenny, some of Ben's difficulties in the speaking task arose from simply trying to understand the interlocutor. Even simple questions like 'Comment t'appelles-tu?' were not immediately recognised if they were not put in the exact form he was used to in school (that is, 'Comment tu t'appelles?'). He explains: 'There, I was baffled again because the question was different so I sort of had to think about it for a minute and then I realised, 'cos that's the thing with speaking, you've got to realise more or less straightaway'. The problems of comprehension are thus compounded by the pressures of supplying an immediate answer. Similarly, when it was his turn to ask the questions, he reported that he was not really listening to the answers as: 'I was just trying to think of what other questions I could ask next . . . and it's going to be a really massive silence and it's going to sound really awful'. Unlike Jenny, he appears not to perceive the interlocutor as an examiner but as someone with whom he is trying to have a 'natural' conversation: 'Cos I know in, like, France . . . they'd like think why are you stopping, it would sound silly to them but it was just thinking time'. He is not yet aware of the use of 'fillers' for this purpose. Time was important for Jenny too but in Ben's case, the need arises not from a concern to monitor but simply: 'Trying to find a word and to look back sort of in my mind'. The 'trawling' process involves recalling what has been learned in school: 'Because recently I've just done holidays I sort of got a rush with different things like swimming, so I could easily think of things to say'. The written word facilitates recall: 'I can just see it written there' and 'I was, like, trying to think in my mind of those pages I drew'. He strings together whatever he can find, omitting articles, pronouns, verbs, and prepositions: 's'appelle Jenny', 'Jane université', 'mmm, je quel âge mm sept ans'. 'Quel âge' operates as an unanalysed *chunk* that is not open to manipulation: 'quel âge vingt-trois, à quel âge dix-neuf'. He can produce correct sentences but only when they have been well rehearsed in school: 'J'ai deux chats et deux chiens'; 'J'aime manger le croissant' – 'we've done that so many times, I was just reeling it off'. Sometimes familiarity interferes with meaning. He explains that he answered 'j'ai deux frères' ('I have two brothers') instead of 'j'ai deux sœurs' ('I have two sisters'), because the question form used in school was 'tu as des frères et des sœurs?' and: 'the first one is frères so I see it first'.

In spite of his very limited linguistic repertoire, he is prepared to take some risks: 'It might work, *c'est grande sœur*' ('it's big sister' for 'it's my older sister'). He exploits the presence of the interlocutor more than Jenny, asking him questions and repeating useful words:

B Je basketball.
I Tu préfères le basket?
B Je préfère le basket.

The overall impression is of a learner seeking to 'make the most of what you've got' (see our discussion of the work of Wong Fillmore in Chapter 2, p. 39) and whose prime aim is to keep the conversation going.

Unlike Jenny, Ben does not appear to profit from the increased space for reflection and analysis offered by the reading task. In terms of top-down processing, he relies primarily on the pictures and the occasional isolated word he recognises to create an initial hypothesis about what the story may be about and ignores any clues to the contrary, inventing a plausible plot that will confirm his initial hypothesis: 'I'm just making it up really'. We will see further examples of this 'wild-card guessing' in Chapter 4. His readiness to skip so much of what he does not recognise means that he invents false connections between isolated sections of the text. Conversely, when he does stop to attempt to analyse a sentence in greater detail, bottom-up processing interferes with the ability to understand the gist of a sentence. He does not appear to be able to identify the essential words that he needs to work on, spending time instead on words like '*son*' in '*son copain*' ('*his* friend') and '*alors*' in 'alors moi' ('*So* I'). He rarely stops to relate his existing linguistic knowledge to the text: '*ils* means "they" and *rester* means, I think, it's "staying" . . . it's not "resting"'. He recognises some cognates (*aventure, danse, arrive*) but not others, initially reading *décider* as *descend*: 'I sort of looked at that quickly and didn't notice there wasn't an "n" in it'. Clues appear to come from the first few letters only and then he makes his guess. The lack of attention to detail and the reluctance to modify an initial hypothesis operates at both word and sentence level. Earlier in his school career, he had difficulties in developing literacy skills in L1. It is possible that the ability to recognise cognates depends on accurate, rapid, reading skills.

Summarising comments

Ben's performance on the two tasks may be typical of a learner at a beginner level. His extensive 'wild-card' guessing and the way he strings words together would suggest an average rather than a proficient learner. The use of unanalysed chunks is a familiar characteristic of a beginner's performance, although proficient learners might be expected in their second year of learning to begin to manipulate them. Like Sophie, his style of learning seems to represent the global/field-dependent learner who prefers social interaction to careful analysis; although it is not clear whether his lack of attention to form also reflects the teaching he is exposed to. This appears to be more in line with the form of communicative language teaching discussed in Chapter 2 than Jenny's experiences of teaching. His level of confidence and concern to 'go for meaning' allows him to maintain a conversation, although not without difficulty. He is not in a position to monitor. The concern to give an impression of himself as capable of carrying on a natural conversation and to avoid silences means that all the mental-processing space is taken up in understanding the interlocutor and in producing some kind of a response: 'to sort of pick my mind'.

Without the presence of an interlocutor to make the use of the language 'real', the reading task becomes a game, leaving him free to invent his own interpretations. It is hard to know the extent to which gender as well as style of learning may also be a factor; whether Ben's performance reflects the 'minimalist' approach associated with boys (see Clark and Trafford 1996) and the lack of confidence in reading even in the L1 (Reynolds 1995).

What are the most useful strategies that would allow Ben to maximise his potential?

Although younger than Sophie and Jenny, Ben is already very aware of how he learns and has surprisingly little difficulty in articulating his thought processes during both tasks. He might then profit from a discussion about how to develop his learning skills. He does not appear to transfer his willingness to 'play with the language' and his enjoyment of the creative aspects of oral tasks to written tasks. Yet like Jenny, he does appear to have useful visual recall of the written word. Time spent generating similar sentences to the written conversations given for homework might facilitate the process of analysing pre-packaged 'chunks'. This might both allow him to express his meanings in conversation more readily and understand varieties of question forms. It might also enable him to recognise what are and are not keywords for reading comprehension. If he had a greater range of reading strategies, he might be less reliant on 'wild-card' guessing. His needs then are the opposite to Jenny in that the strategies he needs to develop are exactly those that she already has (monitoring, paying attention to detail, etc.). Conversely, his confidence and willingness to 'have a go', to recreate a genuine conversation, are exactly the areas that Jenny needs to develop. However, given his difficulties of comprehension, he could be encouraged to see that asking the interlocutor to repeat the question is acceptable: 'I don't know what he spoke about and then he sort of said it slowly and I could hear'.

Conclusion

In this chapter we have set out to describe the profiles of three language learners. We have done so to present what language learning looks like for particular students' practice. Clearly, there are many aspects of what we have discussed which might warrant further detailed attention. We do not have the space to explore every avenue. However, we would like to conclude the chapter by pursuing the theme of *differences* in the learners. First, we look at their individual responses to the speaking task and connect these with their personal cognitive style. Second, and as a follow-up to this focus on speaking, we return to the theoretical issue of the underlying processes involved in managing language. In this case, we connect with our previous discussion of declarative and procedural knowledge and illustrate what this looks like in practice. Third, we add some comments on strategy use in terms of stage of learning and proficiency.

Differences in learners' responses to the speaking task and their cognitive style

Skehan and Foster (1997), in their study, 'Task type and task processing conditions as influences on foreign language performance' gave a series of speaking tasks to students in their early twenties learning English. The speaking tasks were: a personal task, a narrative task and a decision task. They argue that the personal-information task, which required subjects to describe what had most pleasantly or unpleasantly surprised them about life in Britain, would be the least cognitively demanding, because it required subjects to use information that they knew well and had probably rehearsed already in English. Conversely, it may be that for our three school learners of a foreign language, and at an age when they are struggling to establish their own views and identity in L1, conveying personal information in another language is far from straightforward. All three learners reported finding the speaking tasks difficult. Jenny comments on why she prefers the GCSE role-plays to the speaking tasks in this study suggest: 'It just says, like, "Say to the woman that you want a season ticket" – that's easier than here as you're not only trying to think of the French, you're trying to think of the English as well'. Similarly, Sophie explains: 'I just didn't know what to say in English, let alone in French'. It appears as if producing the language, other than through well-rehearsed answers, demands an extensive trawling process and uses up a lot of mental-processing space. Jenny comments: 'I was trying to think of something to say about Daisy, our dog, and I knew that she used to bite everything around the house but I didn't know how to say she used to bite things and I could have said she ate things but that would have changed the meaning'. We will return to this trawling process when we discuss the communication strategy of 'keeping it simple' in Chapter 4 but it seems to entail rapidly answering the following questions before attempting to speak:

1   'What do I remember about this event? What happened? What are my feelings/opinions on this subject?' (Original message to be conveyed.) Sophie's comment: 'I was trying to think of the plot of the play and whether or not it was a tragedy' is similar to Jenny's: 'I didn't know what to say because I couldn't remember why he was wearing a bow tie'.

2   'What of the necessary language do I know? What do I remember of this topic that I have been taught in school?' Ben remembers learning the topic

'holidays'; Jenny explains: 'I was trying to think of things, sort of, like, in the town that relate to topics I did at school as well'. Similarly, Sophie comments: 'And then I was thinking back to being thirteen and doing *en mon jardin, nous avons des arbres et aussi l'herbe*'.

3   'If I can't say what I originally intended, can I alter my original message to incorporate the familiar language?'

4   'If I can't even remember any language from school, have I enough language to attempt another version? What is the simplest way I can do it?'

Within the struggle to communicate, the relationship between the nature of the task, even when it is just concerned with conveying personal information, and the learner's cognitive style may also be significant. Although all of the learners reported difficulties with the speaking task as a whole, they differed in terms of which section of the task they preferred. Both Sophie and Ben found answering the questions harder than discussing the photos. Ben explains his preference for the less-structured photo task thus: 'It was sort of less tight. With the questions there is a direct answer and if I say it wrong then it's wrong'. In contrast, Jenny finds that: 'You've got loads of mess, loads of things going on with a photo and you try to think of something interesting to say but when someone's just asking you a question: it's a lot more standard and I have been asked all the questions and we've practised things like that'. We recognise the difficulty of establishing whether their different approaches to learning and the particular tasks reflect differences in cognitive style, or simply the kind of teaching to which they were exposed. Nevertheless, it seems that Sophie's and Ben's preference for commenting on the photos or asking questions matches their cognitive styles; they welcome the freedom to take control of the topic of conversation and have the social confidence to do so. The same freedom threatens Jenny. The tighter the structure, the safer she feels, as these are predictable routines and she gains her confidence from knowing that she has revised them carefully and can produce the answers accurately. In this context, the 'right answers' that disturb Ben provide her with reassurance.

Differences in declarative and procedural knowledge

In Chapter 2 we discussed the difference between declarative and procedural knowledge as a way of describing the underlying processes of language and language learning. In Figure 2.1 (see p. 45) we used horizontal and vertical axes to express the continua in language processing. We see the map as a way of plotting learner responses. It rejects the notion of a sharp distinction between declarative and procedural knowledge, top-down and bottom-up processing, seeing both instead on a continuum. It also recognises the dynamic nature of the processes involved in dealing with language, allowing us to locate the learner's use of strategies in relation both to each other and to the context.

It is possible to see the declarative–procedural continuum in practice. In the reading task, for example, Sophie proceeds smoothly (procedurally) and deals with the text at a holistic-meaning level until there is a problem. This disruption brings about the application of more declarative knowledge: for example, translation, and a complex web of lexical, syntactic inferencing and monitoring. Similarly, in speaking, she is able to sustain conversation through the use of a whole set of (proceduralised) techniques – pre-packaged forms, fillers, rehearsed topic, etc. For example:

S: J'aime, uh, le sujets que j'avais choisis pour étude pour mon, mes A levels qui sont le dessin, l'anglais et le français.
I1: Uh uh, et qu'est-ce que tu détestes avant que tu . . .
S: Avant, uh, je détestais le mathématiques et puis la chimie.
I2: Les sciences?
S: Les sciences, oui.
I2: Vous aimez les arts?
S: Oui, exactement.

Then she enters an area that is less familiar to her:

I2: Vous allez à l'université l'année prochaine?
S: Oui, je l'espère uh [*sigh*] dans mon, uh, pendant mon année sabbatique, uh, je, je vais étudier le dessin à Camberwell College mais après avoir la fini? J'espère que, uh, il serait possible pour moi, uh, à aller à Sussex.

Here, the pauses are significant. They are suggestive of a kind of grammatical approximation and monitoring taking place. In other words, a 'best attempt' is made at grammatical accuracy and this is held in the mind to be monitored in an explicit way using both conscious and intuitive knowledge. It therefore appears that she is not only monitoring retrospectively, she is also monitoring predictively; in other words, she is aware that a problematic area is coming up for her, which causes her to move out of procedural mode and operate more declaratively. For example, once the problem is dealt with, she returns to procedural mode. Her point of operation is thus continually shifting between declarative and procedural knowledge; and this within a single sentence. This shifting would seem to be true for both speaking and reading. What is clear is that procedural knowledge makes language processing less problematic. The less problematic it is, the more mental space is immediately available to attend to other aspects of the language. In this case, the application of procedural knowledge allows the learner to attend to the finer (style) points of language and be more herself.

We wrote earlier of two distinct senses in which language was problematic: both to deal with specific disruptions in understanding and conveying meaning, and clarifying new responses and ideas in context. Strategies are apparent in both, but they are sequential, they cluster, and are developmentally linked. Moreover, time is an important factor in using them. Generally, proceduralised knowledge buys time, declarative knowledge costs it. Even so, declarative knowledge is the route to procedural knowledge. The objectification of language in this way gains control over it for the learner.

Differences in strategy use, stage of learning and competence

Chesterfield and Chesterfield (1985) argue that strategies should be regarded as developmental: early ones being mainly for receptive skills and self-contained; later ones being more interactive and allowing for greater reflection and meta-reflection in the language task. The picture of the three learners suggests a somewhat more complex path of development, determined by task and cognitive style as well as stage of learning and competence. Chapter 2 discussed the research in relation to these additional factors. As a field-independent learner, Jenny's approach to her learning is different from both Sophie's and Ben's. In spite of being younger than Sophie, she appears to use more complex strategies at least for the learning of grammatical rules and her monitoring, at least in the reading task, is quite sophisticated. Sophie appears to be moving into the 'advanced stage' but a more proficient speaker would be expected to need to monitor less, be less reliant on stock phrases and have fewer occasions where it is necessary to gain control over what is occurring in the conversation, either by attempts to take the initiative in it, to appeal for assistance, or abandon/rephrase an attempted utterance. Ben, also a field-dependent learner, has not embarked on the process of analysing pre-packaged forms. 'Wild-card' guessing is a major feature of his approach to the reading task and he oscillates between this kind of top-down inferencing and word-for-word translation, unable even to identify chunks of meaning.

These case studies of three language learners would seem to suggest that stage alone and competence do not determine the use of strategies, and that learning style and the nature of the task may also be significant factors. Neither Jenny nor Sophie are highly proficient language learners, given their stage of development, each lacking strategies in the one area that the other has, but their strengths allow them a degree of success. It is still too early to identify Ben's potential as a language learner but it is possible that without greater motivation, and clear guidance as to the strategies he needs to develop, he may not be as successful as the other two.

These comments conclude Part One of the book where we have sought to present the case for learning strategies as fruitful and practical descriptions of the process of language acquisition and demonstrate how they might look in theory and practice.

Part Two now takes up the discussion with further extensions of practical matters. Chapter 4 outlines the arguments for intervening and offering learners instruction in the use of new strategies. It also offers some classroom-based materials which could be employed in what might be called *strategy instruction*. Chapter 5 then explores the effects of such strategy instruction in the case of teachers working with them with their pupils. We will see that motivation and learning styles, as well as competence and stage of learning, emerge as significant influences not only on learners' existing use of strategies but also their ability to adopt new strategies.

Part Two

4 Strategy instruction

Introduction: why teach learning strategies?

In this chapter we look at the whole issue of training learners to use more learning strategies. A possible framework or sequence of steps for doing this is offered, along with some practical examples. However, first let us look at the rationale for strategy instruction.

A number of factors have contributed to recent interest in strategy instruction. First, as we have seen in Chapter 2, the close links between learner autonomy and learning strategies have become more and more apparent. More generally, it was perhaps an inevitable consequence of research into learning strategies that it should raise the issue of whether they can or should be taught. If successful learners have a wider repertoire of strategies than their less successful peers, then it seems sensible to intervene and offer them the opportunity to acquire these tools. It could also be argued that making explicit to students how to go about the learning process might not only serve to increase such learners' range of strategies, it might also improve their motivation. Recent developments in attribution theory (see Dickinson 1995) suggest that where learners feel that their lack of success is due to fixed and unchangeable causes, such as their own lack of aptitude or the difficulty of the task, they become readily discouraged. Where they feel the outcome of their learning is not predetermined and they have control over it they tend to persist. Strategies, therefore, could provide learners with one such means of control. As Rubin points out:

> Often poorer learners don't have a clue as to how good learners arrive at their answers and feel that they can never perform as good learners do. By revealing the process, this myth can be exposed.
>
> (1990, p. 282)

Leaving aside differences between successful and less successful learners, there may simply be a case for them to share with each other the strategies that work for them. Low *et al.* (1993) in their study of Scottish primary school pupils learning modern languages noted that, whereas the class as a whole identified a large number of strategies, each individual pupil mentioned only a small number.

Interest in strategy instruction in Britain has also increased, as teachers have got to grips with the National Curriculum. Whereas their initial focus was on covering the topics in the Programme of Study, Part 2 (e.g.: everyday activities, personal and social life, the world around us, the world of work, the international world) more recently attention has turned to the type of teaching and learning opportunities set out in the Programme of Study Part 1 (see the language skills listed in Chapter 2, p. 48). The question here is whether pupils can be expected automatically to: 'acquire strategies for committing familiar language to memory (POS1: 3b)'; 'use context and other clues to interpret meaning (POS1: 3e)'; 'redraft their writing to improve its accuracy and presentation (POS1: 2n)'; or whether it is necessary to make these strategies explicit.

While there may be strong arguments for assuming that strategy instruction would be of use to learners, this is not to say that its potential value is uncontested. Towards the end of the chapter, we will explore some of the issues surrounding this debate, but we will start by presenting concrete examples of what strategy instruction might look like in practice. Implicit in the examples offered here is a certain model of strategy instruction and of its place in the curriculum. Having illustrated this model in some detail, we may then be better placed to consider the theoretical assumptions underlying the model and the questions it raises.

Section 1

How to teach learning strategies – some practical examples of the cycle of strategy instruction in action

There may be considerable discussion about whether strategies should be taught at all and about the place of strategy instruction within the curriculum. Recent years have however seen some consensus emerging on the actual methodology to be used, once a decision has been made to embark on it. O'Malley and Chamot (1990), for example, present a framework of steps common to their own studies and those of Jones *et al.* (1987), Weinstein and Underwood (1985), Hosenfeld *et al.* (1981) and Wenden (1991). The cycle for the illustrations in the following section is based on a similar sequence of steps, as outlined in Harris (1997). The illustrations aim to show how the steps of the cycle can be applied to a range of strategies and across a range of levels. They cover the following areas:

Reading strategies
Listening strategies
Memorisation strategies
Strategies for checking written work
Communication strategies

The first three examples in this chapter are directed towards beginner learners, the last two towards intermediate learners, that is, those with three to four years of language learning. The rationale underlying this selection of particular target groups of learners for particular groups of strategies will be discussed towards the end of the chapter since it raises issues regarding the integration of strategy instruction into the curriculum. Illustrations of the cycle for more advanced learners are not offered since they can be found in publications such as Wenden (1991), O'Malley and Chamot (1990).

Teaching reading strategies
Target Group – year 1–2 of the course

Step 1   Consciousness raising

The purpose of this step is to begin to encourage learners to reflect on the learning process. They are set a task 'cold' and then asked how they went about it, sharing the strategies they used in a class brainstorm. In the case of teaching reading strategies, therefore, the teacher might start by giving pupils a short illustrated book of their choice to read, perhaps for homework. The next day the teacher asks them which strategies they used to work out what it meant and what they did when they came to words or phrases they did not understand. An initial checklist of strategies is drawn up on the board.

This is the point at which the rationale for the intended strategy instruction is explained. It appears to be particularly important to persuade low attainers of the potential value of instruction (O'Malley and Chamot 1990). Although they are the learners for whom it may be most valuable, they may be the least willing to try out new strategies, feeling that they will 'never be any good at foreign languages'. In order to improve their motivation, it is worth convincing them that the difficulties they have experienced so far may be due to lack of strategies, rather than lack of ability.

Step 2   Modelling

The class brainstorm will have already allowed learners to begin to share the strategies that work for them. But in the next step, the teacher may need to model others that are less familiar. Figure 4.1, a Dutch poem, can provide a context where the class collectively translates what they can and the teacher illustrates how other strategies can be brought into play to decipher the rest. (A translation is provided at the end of this chapter.)

The translation of the poem is likely to engage the class in discussing at least some of the following strategies. Additions may be made to the initial checklist:

- recognising the type of text (a poem for children) and therefore having some expectations of what it might be about;
- going for gist – skipping non-essential words;
- using the title and the pictures for clues (it is likely that not all the learners will have noticed the pictures behind the little girl);

Éen appel is rood,
de zon is geel,
de hemel is blauw,
een blad is groen,
een wolk is wit . . .
en de aarde is bruin.

Én zou je nu kunnen
antwoorden
op de vraag . . .

Welke Kleur de liefde?

Figure 4.1 Dutch poem

- identifying 'chunk boundaries' – how a text breaks down and which parts of it to work on at any one time;
- using common sense and knowledge of the world (earth is not blue);
- looking for cognates;
- saying the text out loud;
- using the pattern of sentences to make sensible guesses ('a something is + colour');
- breaking down an unknown word/phrase and associating parts of it with familiar words;
- using punctuation for clues; questions marks, capital letters, etc.;
- identifying the grammatical category of words.

The extent to which the last strategy is explored will depend on the level of the class and the need for the particular strategy in establishing comprehension of the text. For some tasks, identifying the tense marker may be essential for comprehension; for others, spotting adverbs such as 'yesterday', 'tomorrow' may be sufficient.

The order in which the reading strategies above are presented is intended to reflect a broad continuum, described in Chapter 2; starting from those that might be associated with 'top-down' processing (global comprehension of the text as a whole) to those indicative of a 'bottom-up' approach (word-for word 'decoding').

Step 3   General practice

It will be clear from discussions elsewhere in the book that it is unrealistic to assume that simply telling students about possible fruitful strategies will ensure that these pass into their repertoire and can be drawn on automatically. Explicit reminders to use the reading strategies will be necessary alongside a number of tasks and materials likely to promote them. Learners can first be presented with materials which make explicit the relationship between sections of the text and the particular strategies that could be used, as in the example in Figure 4.2 from Harris (1997). In reading subsequent texts, learners may still need a focused reminder to use the strategies. Table 4.1, adapted from Swarbrick (1990), is one attempt to do this.

The pupil using this worksheet only employed the one strategy of 'guessing' and consistently guessed incorrectly. Like Ben, in Chapter 3, he appears to use 'wild-card' guessing, writing down the first thing that comes into his head, often based on the use of the single strategy of cognates. It might be that if he were encouraged first to try out some of the other strategies on the list, his guesses would become more accurate. As we have previously mentioned, it is often the ability to use a combination of strategies that characterises the successful learner.

Step 4   Action planning; goal setting and monitoring

Donato and McCormick (1994) report on a project they undertook where learners had to keep a portfolio in which they provided concrete self-selected evidence of their growing language abilities; using it as a benchmark to thinking about performance, planning future courses of action and monitoring their accomplishments. While their project involved advanced learners, the 'action plan' in Table 4.2 on page 80 might help even beginner learners to identify their own targets, the particular strategies that will help to achieve them and the means by which they will measure success.

However, learners may need some help in identifying which strategies are most appropriate to their goals and their level. It is likely that different types of text will involve the use of different strategies and it cannot be assumed that they will perceive the most appropriate strategies for each text type. A study by Thompson and Rubin (1996) on the effects of teaching listening strategies suggests the importance of the type of listening text. Similar considerations may well apply for reading. Even beginner learners have some choice in what they read, selecting from 'book boxes' of illustrated short stories, holiday brochures, extracts from magazines or letters from an exchange school. In some cases the published materials (see for example the *Bibliobus* and *Lesekiste* series published by Mary Glasgow) cover a range of different types of 'short books'; from those which tell a story, to those which provide factual information about scientific discoveries, for example, or about famous people. While pictures may provide useful clues for reading magazine articles, cartoons or recipes, they will not always be available; for example, when reading letters. 'Using your common sense' may be a strategy

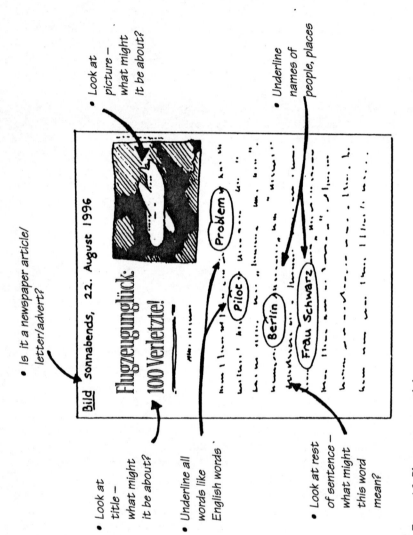

Figure 4.2 Plane picture worksheet

Table 4.1 My word discoveries

Learning words through reading								
German	*Looks like English*	*Guessed*	*Used word list*	*Carried on reading*	*Picture helped*	*Asked another student*	*Used dictionary*	**English**
Teufelstich		✓						Boat
Birgit		✓						Bright
machen		✓						Match
Strandbad		✓						Sand

Table 4.2 Action plan for developing reading skills

Action Plan	
Name:	
I want to be able to	*read articles in real French teenagers' magazines*
I have selected the following strategies	*looking for cognates, using the title and pictures for clues*
I will know I have improved because	*I won't give up half-way through the article and I won't have to look up so many words*

that can be drawn on in reading a story but might be harder when trying to follow a scientific explanation. Making explicit the links between strategies and tasks may be the first step in arriving at appropriate, personal goals.

Step 5   *Focused practice and fading out the reminders*

After learners have drawn up their own individual action plan, opportunities are provided for them to pursue it. Learners interested in reading similar types of text can be encouraged to work together in pairs or groups and further texts can be set for homework. Explicit directions to use particular strategies, in the form of checklists or worksheets, are gradually faded out, until students are simply reminded to use the strategies they have previously identified. The aim is that they should reach a stage where they have successfully internalised the strategies and can draw on them automatically, without prompting from the teacher. It may again be helpful to consider the process as analogous to driving a car. Initially, we may need the instructor to give explicit directions for changing gears – look in the mirror, reduce your speed, put your foot on the clutch, etc. – but finally, the steps involved have to become an automatic response. Much of the skill of the teacher lies in judging how and when these reminders can be progressively faded out.

Step 6   *Evaluating strategy acquisition and recommencing the cycle*

The teacher seeks to withdraw gradually the supportive scaffolding provided by the reminders and to establish whether the strategies have been assimilated and can be deployed effectively. The most appropriate moment to do this will vary from learner to learner and will be a matter for the teacher's professional judgement. The use of an action plan also allows the learner to play an active role in this process; discussing if the anticipated progress has been made. If it has not, then teacher and learner can establish what is going wrong and agree possible solutions, which then form the basis of the next action plan. If it has, they can devise a new action plan and the cycle recommences with a new focus. This may include expanding the range of reading of different types of text (poetry, newspaper articles, short stories, etc.), or simply a more detailed understanding of the existing type of text.

It is for the teacher to determine the scope of the goals adopted by learners in the action-planning step and to direct them accordingly. We will see some examples in the rest of the chapter. Teachers may choose to limit the focus of an action plan to:

- the attainment of the learners – moving, for example, from simply memorising the meaning of words to also remembering their spelling and gender;
- the problems learners face in a particular skill area – learners like Jenny have different communication difficulties to learners like Sophie;
- varying the type of text;
- varying the type of task;
- helping learners to select the most appropriate strategies for the text or task.

We have outlined a cycle of six steps in relation to the teaching of reading strategies. The steps were as follows:

1 Consciousness/Awareness raising;
2 Modelling;
3 General practice;
4 Action planning;
5 Focused practice;
6 Evaluation.

We now want to show how a similar sequence of steps can be adopted for teaching learners other skill strategies. We begin with listening.

Teaching listening strategies

Target group – 1–2 years of the course

It will not be surprising to find similarities between activities for teaching reading strategies and those for teaching listening strategies, since both involve similar processes. Listening, however, may place more demands on the learner since:

- learners have no visual clues, unless a video recording is used;
- learners are not supported by the written word and must therefore break the stream of sound down into individual words for themselves;
- learners do not have time to reflect on the meaning unless the recording is played a number of times. Even then it is more fleeting than reading a text.

Effective listening may depend on the use of the following strategies. The order in which they are presented seeks to reflect a continuum from 'top-down' to 'bottom-up' processing:

Table 4.3 Listening strategies

Listening
1 Recognising the type of listening text; conversation/advert/news programme?
2 Recognising the topic; going for gist.
3 Guessing on the basis of knowledge of the world; what is likely/unlikely in this situation? Using common sense.
4 Using the tone of speakers' voices for clues (and facial gestures in the case of video).
5 Picking out cognates.
6 Identifying unfamiliar phrases and playing the relevant section of the tape over and over again.
7 Holding the unfamiliar sounds in your head; saying them over and over again.
8 Trying to break down the stream of sound into individual words.
9 Trying to write the sounds down and to relate them to written words previously learned.
10 Listening out for clues from the tense, word order, etc.

Since ready access to the use of videos is limited in many classrooms, the cycle will be illustrated using audio recordings, as in Table 4.4.

The cycle will next be illustrated by discussing strategies to memorise vocabulary or grammar rules, a task often assigned for 'homework'.

Teaching memorisation strategies

Target group – 1–2 years of the course

Learning that takes place outside the confines of the classroom is an important element of developing autonomy and the application of strategies. Adult learners have long been encouraged to develop individual study plans for within and outside the classroom based on their personal needs (see Dickinson 1987, Sheerin 1989, Wenden 1991, Broady and Kenning 1996). Where learners are living within the target-language community, their plans may include opportunities to meet native speakers, watch television, etc. The scope to develop such ideas with secondary school learners appears to be more limited.

Table 4.4 Cycle of strategy instruction: listening

Stage in cycle	Activity
1 Awareness raising	Learners are set a listening task 'cold', i.e. not told anything about the context. But they are reminded that this may be a situation they encounter in 'real life'; e.g. eavesdropping on a conversation in a bus, or switching on the radio. They discuss what they did and did not understand and the class brainstorms the strategies they used. An initial checklist is drawn up.
2 Modelling	
Identifying the type of text	Learners listen to various short snippets of text. At first, the teacher provides the options: Is it a conversation between friends? A news report? An advert? Teacher encourages learners to use clues such as tone of voice, speed of delivery, jingles, etc. The teacher then plays more snippets, without providing any options, and learners compete to identify the type of text.
Identifying the topic	The teacher now asks learners to identify the topic of the snippets. Again at first the teacher provides the options: Is it an advert for a record shop, for a soap powder or for dog food? For each snippet, pupils list any keywords they recognise, to discover the likely topic, e.g. 'eat', 'dog', 'healthy'.
Prediction and comparison and *identifying familiar words and cognates*	Having identified the various topics, the teacher now focuses on one particular snippet and the class works through various steps together under the teacher's guidance. They brainstorm in the first language all the words and expressions they can predict might be said in that situation. They then brainstorm all the words on the topic in the target language with which they are already familiar, matching them, where possible, to the first language list on the board.
	Now learners listen again for the words that are actually said. One learner comes up to the board and ticks the words mentioned. Another has the task of adding any other familiar phrases or cognates that they recognise. The teacher may also stop the tape at certain moments and ask learners to predict what comes next.
Using common sense	The next step is 'Listen again and guess'. Having identified some of the key familiar words, learners are asked to use their common sense to guess the meaning of the less familiar ones. The teacher may stop the tape at appropriate moments. It may be worth first giving some examples: a waiter asks them something and the only word they recognise is the verb to drink. What is he likely to be asking? A nonsense text in English (e.g. Lewis Carroll's 'Twas brillig and the slithy toves') may enable pupils to see how much can be guessed from the context and grammatical clues.

Table 4.4 continued

Stage in cycle	Activity
Saying over and over/writing down sounds	The next steps are based on identifying and solving remaining problems. Learners may raise their hand when they come to something they do not understand. The teacher plays the section again; learners have one minute to say the sounds over to themselves and/or try to write them down. In languages like Spanish and German, the relationship between the spoken and the written form may be relatively straightforward. In French and English, learners may need some practice before the strategy instruction commences in associating particular written forms to their sound. 'Nation' and 'formation' in French are not readily recognisable as cognates to English speakers, if they are not aware '-tion' is pronounced like 'shun'. Rendall (1998) suggests a range of useful activities for developing this strategy.
Using clues from grammatical endings and word order	Spot the difference! Before the strategy instruction commences, the teacher may first want to practise paying particular attention to hearing slight differences in sounds, e.g. *ich spiele, ich spielte* (I play, I played), *les cheveux, les chevaux* (hair, horses). The teacher can refer back to it, when he or she says the sections that are still not understood and writes them on the board. Depending on the level of the class and the importance of the particular grammatical feature for comprehension, it may be appropriate to alert students to clues from word order, tense, etc.
Reviewing	Finally, learners are given the transcript and asked if they can work out the meaning of anything else they have not understood. They could be asked which strategies they could have used to help them earlier, so that they become more aware of their own individual patterns of strategy use.
3 **General practice**	Although the steps in the modelling process may have to be repeated a number of times with different recordings, as soon as possible, learners need to work in small groups rather than as a whole class. This allows them to control which section of the tape to play again, to pool ideas for familiar language and to use the strategies for themselves. The work sheet in Figure 4.3 on page 86 is one which serves to remind them of the steps outlined in the modelling process.
4 **Action planning**	Unlike reading, learners often have very little choice in what they listen to so the action plan in Table 4.5 on page 87 may have to be less specific, based on an awareness of their own general difficulties, rather than interest in a particular type of listening text. This does however suggest the need to create more opportunities where learners can select from a range of listening materials on the basis of interest (e.g. pop songs,

Table 4.4 continued

Stage in cycle	Activity
	interviews with sports stars, recipes, radio jingles). In that case, they would need support in identifying the most appropriate strategies for the particular genre chosen.
5 Focused practice and fading out the reminders	The checklists or directed worksheets are withdrawn and pupils are simply reminded to use the strategies for subsequent listening tasks.
6 Evaluating strategy acquisition and recommencing the cycle	At some point, the teacher will wish to ascertain whether the strategies have been internalised so that a new action plan can be drawn up. The initial goal for a low-attaining learner to get the gist of the recording may shift to focusing on a more detailed understanding by saying the words over and over and trying to write them down. As previously noted for strategy instruction in reading strategies, the teacher may also want to draw learners' attention to the relationship between the type of listening task set and the most useful strategies to achieve a successful outcome, and, subsequently may wish to provide practice in matching tasks to strategies.

Dam (1995, p. 33) describes how in her classes in Denmark each learner chooses the homework they will undertake, supported by a general list of possible tasks previously compiled as a whole-class activity. While similar homework practices have been employed within the British context (Page 1992), it is more frequently the case that learners have little choice in the tasks they undertake. Often, they are simply asked to learn a certain number of words for their home-work. Although storage and rapid retrieval of vocabulary is indispensable for successful language learning and use, the assumption is made that learners are aware of how to go about the memorisation process efficiently. But even quite advanced learners may assume that copying down lists of vocabulary or grammar rules will somehow ensure that they pass, by osmosis, into their heads.

Oxford (1990) identifies four sets of memory strategies:

- creating mental linkages;
- applying images and sounds;
- reviewing well;
- employing action.

Each of the sets is subdivided into related strategies. Common to them all is Oxford's assertion (ibid., p. 39) that:

for the purpose of learning a language, the arrangements and associations must be personally meaningful to the learner and the material to be reviewed must have significance.

1   What *type of text* is it?   conversation/news report/advert

2   What is the main *topic*?   record shop/soap powder/dog food

3   *Predict* what could be said and *compare* to what you hear on the tape

What words are likely to be said? (English)	What is the French for these words?	Tick if you heard them	Other words we recognised

4   Play it again. Use your *common sense*: is there anything else you can guess now?

5   Problems? Play it again: what words or phrases do you still not understand? *Say the sounds over and over*; can you write any of them down?

Can you guess anything more from clues from the ends of words or the word order?

6   Look at the transcript. Underline the sections you still don't understand. Can you work out what they mean now? Are there any strategies that could have helped you work them out earlier?

I could have used the strategy of . . . to guess . . .

Figure 4.3 Learning to listen (referred to on p. 84)

Table 4.5 Action plan for developing listening skills (referred to on p. 84)

Action Plan	
Name:	
I want to be able to	*understand the rough idea of what is being said*
I have selected the following strategies	*using the tone of voice, predicting what is likely to be said in that situation*
I will know I have improved because	*I won't panic when I first hear something I don't understand*

She suggests that the strategy of structured reviewing is of particular importance since it helps move information from the 'fact' level to the 'skill' level, 'where knowledge is more procedural and automatic'. It is thus more easily retrieved and less easily lost after a period of disuse. Differences in learning style may mean that some strategies are more useful for one learner than another. While some learners, like Sophie, benefit from visual imagery, others have aural, kinaesthetic or tactile learning preferences. A scheme for a cycle of strategy instruction in memorisation is presented below.

Table 4.6 Cycle of strategy instruction: memorisation

Stage in cycle	Activity
1 **Awareness raising**	Learners are presented with the familiar homework task of learning a certain number of items of vocabulary. The next lesson, the teacher brainstorms with the learners how they went about their homework and collects their ideas on the board in the form of a checklist. The checklist may be added to after the 'modelling' stage.
2 **Modelling**	The teacher models some of the strategies, learners others. It may not be obvious, for example, how to develop a 'photographic memory' or what is involved in 'mind maps' (Figure 4.4) on page 89. Examples of word and visual association may need to be provided. The picture in Figure 4.5 on page 90 illustrates the Spanish word for alarm clock (*despertador*). Word association of 'spurting to the door' when the alarm goes off creates a visual image. A checklist can then be drawn up; the example in Figure 4.6 on page 91 was devised by Angelina Adams, one of the teachers whose experiences are described in the next chapter.

continued . . .

Table 4.6 continued

Stage in cycle	Activity
3 General practice	Initially, learners may need allocated classroom time to become familiar with the strategies. Space can be created during lessons for learners to try out different strategies, to evaluate them in terms of preference, and to give reasons for their preferences. For example, the class has to learn a further group of items but this time they work in groups. Each group is assigned a particular strategy. The groups then compare their experiences. Or the task can be completed in pairs, but each learner has to try out the other's preferred memorisation strategies and comment on them. In subsequent learning-homework tasks, learners are reminded to tick off the strategies they tried on their checklist to ensure that they are still practising them.
4 Action planning	In devising their action plan, (Table 4.7 on page 90), learners may need some help in identifying which strategies are most appropriate to their goals. Not all of them will be aware that while writing the words down may improve their spelling, it will do little to enhance their pronunciation or to help them recall the meaning. Making explicit the links between strategies and their associated skills may promote their understanding of the learning process.
5 Focused practice and fading out the reminders	Opportunities for further practice of memorisation strategies can be readily integrated into the lesson, offering simple ways of providing differentiation. Even though some of the class may not have completed a speaking task or a written worksheet, those who have can move on to identifying the words they found hardest to remember and using the strategies on their action plan to learn them. Finally, pupils are simply reminded to use the strategies they have selected to learn any new words.
6 Evaluating strategy acquisition and recommencing the cycle	It is for the teacher to decide at what point to ascertain whether the strategies have been internalised so that a new action plan can be drawn up. A low-attaining learner, for example, may have initially aimed simply at remembering the meaning of the words; subsequent goals may focus on spelling, pronunciation or gender.

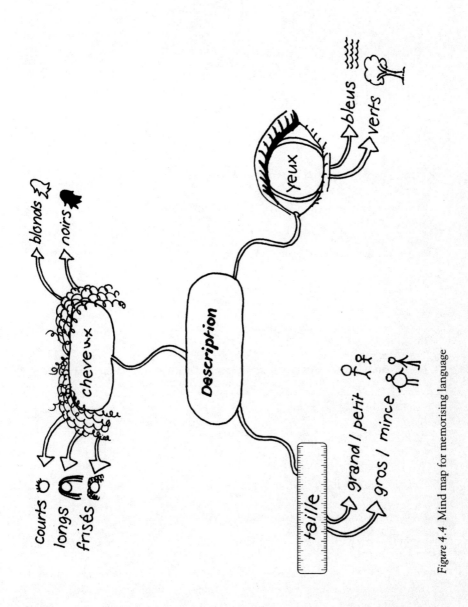

Figure 4.4 Mind map for memorising language

Figure 4.5 Visual association for memorising language

The next examples are geared towards intermediate rather than beginner learners.

Table 4.7 Action plan for developing memorisation skills

Action Plan	
Name:	
I want to be able to	*improve my pronunciation*
I have selected the following strategies	*listening to the tape and repeating the words out loud*
I will know I have improved because	*I will sound more French, I won't hesitate so much in role-plays*

Teaching how to check written work

Target group: 3–4 years of the course

A frequent source of frustration for many teachers is learners' apparent inability to check their work and to engage effectively in the drafting and redrafting process. The advent of coursework as an element of the GCSE examination in Britain has made teachers increasingly concerned to improve learners' ability to check their own work. While they can give feedback to learners when they are planning their coursework essay, they are not allowed to do so once the process of writing has begun. It is often difficult to understand why learners fail to spot

Nom:	Classe:	Cochez
1. Lisez les mots à haute voix		
2. Lisez les mots en silence plusieurs fois		
3. Couvrez les mots		
4. Faites-vous tester		
5. Concentrez-vous sur les mots difficiles		
6. Ecrivez les mots		
7. Répétez les mots rythmiquement		
8. Ecoutez		
9. Enregistrez-vous		
10. Rappelez-vous ce qu'a dit le professeur		
11. Cherchez les indices		
12. Faites rimer les mots		
13. Vouloir apprendre		
14. 'Déballez' les mots		
15. Inventez une chanson		

Figure 4.6 Checklist for memorising language (devised by Angelina Adams)

mistakes on their own, yet once the teacher has pointed to the particular word or group of words, they are able to recognise the problem. Learners' difficulties in checking their work become more understandable if the complex processes involved are analysed. In fact, successful linguists often read and reread their work, using different strategies each time. We can draw on O'Malley and Chamot's taxonomy (1990) to identify the most relevant:

1 Sense monitoring: 'does it make sense?'
2 Auditory monitoring: 'does it sound right?'
3 Visual monitoring: 'does it look right?'
4 Style monitoring: 'is this appropriate?'
5 Paying attention to familiar grammatical mistakes: 'I usually forget to make the adjectives agree with the gender of the nouns'.
6 Problem identification: 'I am not sure if this is right'.
7 Resourcing: knowing where and how to look things up in a dictionary or grammar reference book.

Strategies 2 and 3 in Figure 4.8 only work because learners have built up some familiarity with the language, often at an unconscious level. Hence, in our first language, we may sometimes write down two alternative spellings of a word (e.g. accommodation/ accomodation, solicitor/sollicitor) to see which 'looks right'. Similarly, in a second language we may say over to ourselves 'je suis allé', 'j'ai allé' to check which version sounds the most familiar. While beginners can be encouraged to develop this 'sense', systematic instruction of these strategies seems more appropriate for intermediate learners. Table 4.8 suggests ways in which the cycle of strategy instruction can be used to encourage learners to develop the strategies needed to check their work. The language to be learned in this case is German.

Table 4.8 Cycle of strategy instruction: writing

Stage in cycle	Activity
1 **Awareness-raising**	Class is given homework over holidays of writing an essay on 'An enjoyable/disastrous weekend'. Lesson begins by asking learners to spend 5 minutes checking their work, then to check their friend's. Class brainstorms how they go about checking work and an initial checklist of strategies is drawn up. The checklist may be added to after the 'modelling' stage. Discussion about the value of checking each other's work, looking 'with fresh eyes', may help learners to appreciate the importance of letting a certain amount of time elapse before they check their work.
2 **Modelling**	
Does it make sense?	Class is given text and asked to check it. Text includes contradictory statements such as 'Ich bin Einzelkind' ('I am

Table 4.8 continued

Stage in cycle	Activity
	an only child') and then later on in the same paragraph 'Mein Bruder spielt gern Fussball' ('my brother likes playing football'). When learners realise that the errors do not lie in punctuation or spelling, it can be pointed out that it is not possible to look for such errors and at the content all at once in the first reading.
Does it look right?	Pairs of learners are given a list of words and asked to circle the correct version e.g.: Schwimmbad Schwimbad geradaus geradeaus
Does it sound right?	Teacher reads aloud passage with deliberate mistakes in word order or plural forms, etc. Learners have to raise hand every time they spot one.
Style and content	Learners read two letters and have to pick out the best and say why.
Problem identification, paying attention to familiar grammatical mistakes and *resourcing*	Class is given passage to read and correct, and then brainstorm most usual mistakes. List includes use of *haben* or *sein* as the past auxiliary, capital letters, word order, adjectival endings, etc. Next to each item, learners make a note of any relevant page references from their textbook, grammar book, etc.
3 General Practice	Learners write down paragraph with five deliberate errors. Given to friend to correct for homework.
Reviewing	Learners read aloud to each other the redrafted version of their essay. This may not only practise 'does it sound right?' but also enhance awareness of style, e.g.: 'Does it flow? Is there any repetition? Have good linking-words and advanced phrases been used?' Learners examine friend's further redrafted version of essay and assign it a mark for language content and another mark for accuracy. Learners rewrite essay using checklist of points to bear in mind. (See Figure 4.7, which was devised by Linsey Hand (a trainee teacher) while working with a Year-10 class.)
4 Action planning	Final draft of essay is marked by teacher and returned. Learners write down a list of their own weaknesses and of useful strategies to help to overcome them for next piece of coursework e.g. *'spelling: to use a dictionary when I am unsure or it does not look right'.* Teacher adds her own suggestions to learners' list.

Table 4.8   continued

Stage in cycle	Activity
5 Focused practice and fading out the reminders	Learners complete Table 4.9 after each subsequent homework so that they continue to focus on using the strategies. After some time has elapsed, the class is simply reminded to check their work carefully.
6 Evaluating strategy acquisition and recommencing the cycle	Learner and teacher evaluate success of action plans and a new plan is devised. A high-attaining learner, for example, may be encouraged to widen their stylistic repertoire. A low-attaining learner may need to continue to focus on familiar grammatical mistakes.

Table 4.9 Errors identified on focused rereading of homework

Strategy	One mistake I corrected
1 Does it make sense?	
2 Does it sound right?	
3 Does it look right?	
4 Checking for my most usual mistakes:	
• •	
5 Is the style right?	
6 Looked up	
7 What I am still unsure of	
• Put a star by the special strategies you chose for your action plan	

Teaching communication strategies

Target group: 3–4 years of the course

In Chapter 2 we referred to communication strategies as those techniques used in face-to-face conversations. Some communication strategies may be relatively easy to teach to beginners. Non-verbal strategies such as *mime* are an obvious example, although it is curious that relatively few teachers appear to positively encourage it or set up situations which require it. A colleague of ours successfully explained to a campsite manager in France that there was a bees' nest next to her tent by saying 'près tente, il y a . . .' ('near tent, there is . . .') and then

Checklist! ☺ ☺

1 Read through and check for content

   Have you included everything that was in your plan? Are
   there any inconsistencies? ☐

2 Look at the style and use of language

   Have you chosen the correct language for the task? Does
   the writing 'flow'? Have you used linking-words? ☐

3 Read the passage once more. Does it look right?

   Look for spellings, punctuation, layout, missed umlauts
   or umlauts where there should not be any and don't
   forget: **capital letters on all nouns!** ☐

4 Read the passage aloud. Does it sound right?

   Listen to the word order. Are any words missing? Does
   the grammar 'feel' right? (e.g. have you used the correct
   auxiliary – 'haben'/'sein'? Are the adjectival endings correct?
   Have you chosen the correct gender? Have you sent the
   verb to the end when using 'weil'?) ☐

5 Read **at least** once more to check the fine details

   Have you repeated yourself or used one particular word
   too often? Is there a logical progression of ideas and
   information? Have you made any typing errors? Are there
   any words which you need to look up? Have you used any
   anglicised words or words from another language which
   can be replaced with more authentic German words? ☐

Figure 4.7 Checklist for reviewing writing.

making a buzzing noise, while bringing her finger up to her arm and 'stinging' it. Such situations would allow learners to draw on the language they do know as well as using their imagination to mime what they do not. Beginner learners can also be encouraged to 'make the most of what they have got' by the use of *intonation*, even if the patterns are somewhat different in the target language. They can, for example, act out a basic dialogue where names and family details are exchanged in the style of two famous people; or a type of film (horror, romance, etc.); or according to a particular context ('Lost child', 'Someone who has amnesia', etc.). *Word coinage*, saying the word in English but with a French/German/Spanish accent, should also be within their grasp. They might first be asked to describe or imitate how well-known foreign television personalities sound when they are speaking English to help them identify typical pronunciation patterns. This can also help to develop the awareness of the differences between how a word is said and how it is written, discussed earlier under 'Listening strategies'.

The teaching of other more complex communication strategies, however, may be more appropriate for learners who have a wider linguistic repertoire. *Circumlocution*, for example, implies that the learner has a stock of basic vocabulary on which to draw in order to describe the object. In the example of the bees' nest, the colleague would have needed to know words like insect, yellow, sting, home, etc. The use of communication strategies is also particularly challenging, once we begin to reflect on the affective and temporal demands that communication imposes on the learner. The fact that in mid-flow of a conversation we can find ourselves 'lost for words' demands a certain level of both confidence and competence to 'think round the problem' and arrive at a solution in a matter of seconds. It is unsurprising to find that research evidence (Bialystock 1990) suggests that where communication strategies such as circumlocution are taught to learners, the take-up is disappointing.

Some learners may not be particularly good 'conversationalists', even in their first language, and may find it difficult to keep a conversation going. They may be unfamiliar with the *turn-taking gambits* discussed by Johnstone (1989, p. 160). These include *turn-getting gambits* to break into a conversation, ('No, but listen', 'Yes, but . . . ') and *turn-giving gambits* to invite participation from others ('Isn't it?', 'Don't you think?'). These turn-giving strategies also include encouraging the addressee to say more ('Yes, I see'; 'How interesting'), thus relieving the pressure to talk oneself. As we saw in Chapter 3 in relation to Jenny, they are particularly useful for keeping a conversation going, when your own linguistic resources are very limited. There is some evidence to suggest that males (Spender 1980) may be reluctant to use turn-giving strategies even in their first language and are more comfortable with turn-getting strategies, including manipulating the conversation towards topics with which one is familiar ('By the way'; 'Talking of . . . '; 'Have you heard that. . .?'). The strategy of *topic manipulation* is a valuable means of maintaining the conversation and control over what is discussed.

Learners may also not have appreciated how much can be gained simply by *listening carefully to the interlocutor's language* and using it for oneself. We saw in Part One, for example, how Sophie 'picked up on' expressions used by the interviewer and used them later for herself. An astute listener often also notes the tense used by the native speaker and the correct form of the verb, and then repeats it in their own utterances. Finally, some learners may not realise that it is perfectly acceptable (if somewhat frustrating) to considerably modify what one originally intended to say. They may need, however, some support in practising how such adjustments may be made rapidly. *Keeping it simple* may be an obvious strategy to a successful linguist but, as was noted for strategies for checking written work, it implies the application of a number of other strategies:

- identifying various possible levels for conveying the message from the 'bare bones' needed to get the basic message across to a more sophisticated and detailed version;
- trawling through what they have already learned in order to identify what resources are at their disposal, as Ben did in Chapter 3;
- identifying gaps in their linguistic repertoire and then making a decision as to whether they have the means to use other strategies such as circum-locution;
- making a final decision as to the level of the message they will attempt, having rapidly matched up each level to their own resources.

To give an anecdotal example, on a recent trip to Mallorca one of us wanted to explain to the taxi driver in Spanish something along the lines of: 'Don't bother to take us all the way back to the hotel. You can just drop us on the main road nearby as we want to eat out at a restaurant before going home'. Realising that most of the vocabulary was unknown, the eventual utterance was: 'Here is good. We are going to eat'. Despite its limited nature, it did succeed in conveying the message. Although beginner learners will need to be exposed to the strategy of 'keeping it simple', it may be the case that it is the intermediate learners who need most support with the strategy. Beginners may accept that what they can say will be extremely restricted at first. Intermediate learners may feel a sense of frustration that after three to four years of learning the language, they still cannot express themselves as they would like and that somehow this implies 'failure'. As we have noted in the case of Ben in Chapter 3, this may be true particularly for adolescent learners, who are keen to assert their identity as adults in the new language.

Two further strategies were noted on the same Mallorca trip. The first was a 'filler', or rather a way of *keeping the conversation going*. Having learned expressions for the weather, it was surprising how easily they could be slotted into most conversations. It might be worthwhile teachers identifying a similar ubiquitous topic for adolescent learners. The second relates to 'make the most of what you have got' and *pre-packaged chunks*. The Spanish for 'is it possible . . .?' was used to generate sentences as diverse as: to sit by the window/to hire a car/to phone England/to smoke in the restaurant, etc.

In illustrating the cycle of strategy instruction, we will focus on some of the more complex communication strategies. The list is by no means comprehensive and other strategies such as 'adopting a suitable register', will need to be taught:

- keeping it simple.
- keeping it going:
  - turn-taking and turn-giving gambits
  - topic manipulation
  - 'fillers'
  - circumlocution
  - picking up on the interlocutor's expression.

The cycle is particularly difficult to implement for communication strategies, given that learners may need extensive exposure to the strategies before they can be expected to produce them in spontaneous speech. Therefore, the use of audio and video recordings may be necessary. Classroom conditions may also militate against the extensive oral practice needed. As the only 'native speaker', the classroom teacher cannot provide sufficient one-to-one practice for each learner.

Given these difficulties, it is probably wisest to focus on only one or two of the communication strategies at a time. The context for the first illustration of the cycle (Table 4.10) is 'Booking a room at a hotel'. Since the transactional nature of this task does not lend itself very readily to turn-getting gambits, the second example (Table 4.11) focuses on 'Arranging an outing with a friend'. The assumption is that the steps: awareness raising, action planning and fading out reminders suggested in the first example will also apply to the second.

It is assumed that some of the activities for 'keeping it simple' used in Table 4.10 could also be integrated into this task. The main focus here is on 'keeping it going' through topic manipulation, turn-getting and turn-giving gambits.

Section 2

How to teach learning strategies – some theoretical considerations

A number of practical examples of the cycle of strategy instruction have been presented in this chapter – the 'how' of teaching strategies. What theoretical assumptions lie behind the model proposed? Common to them all is a view that training in strategy use should not be a 'bolt-on' addition to an otherwise traditional classroom but should support the development of communicative competence and learner autonomy. We have already indicated in Chapter 2 the inextricable links between the three areas. In this section, we want to further develop the argument by examining some guiding principles for teaching learning strategies. We will then conclude the chapter with a return to some of the issues and justifications surrounding strategy instruction.

Table 4.10 Cycle of strategy instruction: communication strategies (illus. 1)

Booking in at a hotel room	
Stage in cycle	*Activity*
1 Awareness-raising	Learners perform in pairs the communicative task of booking a room at a hotel. The task is given 'cold', i.e. it has not been prepared in previous lessons. They must convey as much information as possible using whatever means are at their disposal. Conversations are recorded so that at a later date learners can identify the strategies on which they most need to work. The class brainstorms the strategies used, and pairs may 'model' for the class the strategies they adopted. An initial checklist of communication strategies is drawn up. The checklist may be added to after the subsequent 'modelling' stage.
2 Modelling	
Keeping it simple	There may be some value in giving learners a passage in their first language related to hotel bookings (e.g. a request from a manager asking the secretary to make the necessary arrangements) and asking them to turn it into 'telegraphese' or a message to be left on an 'ansaphone'. This may help them to see which language elements are indispensable and which are less important. Variations in the constraints given (20–50 words, 30 seconds–1 minute 'ansaphone' time) might allow them to see the difference between 'bare bones' and more sophisticated messages. They could also listen to non-native speakers giving a 'bare-bones' message in another language and identify the more sophisticated message originally intended. They might then be asked to list all the words they know in the target language for booking a hotel room for each level of message, using textbooks, etc., to remind them of topics covered. Having identified the 'gaps', they could then move on to exploring if other communication strategies such as circumlocution might allow them to be filled.
Keeping it going: circumlocution	Initial tasks focusing on circumlocution may ask the learners to guess the word from a simple description in the target language (where you sleep; bed, where you wash your body but not a bath; shower). Subsequent modelling requires learners to spot the strategies used on audio or video recordings, where perhaps a non-native speaker is asking a native speaker for a hotel room. After first listening to the recording to identify as many examples of the strategy as they can, learners can then be given the transcript to analyse in more detail. They might then be asked to supply alternative forms of circumlocution to those used by the non-native speaker.

continued

Table 4.10 continued

Stage in cycle	Activity
Keeping it going: fillers *and* picking up on *expressions used*	Initial tasks for modelling 'fillers' might require them to perform the hotel-booking conversation in their first language and make a note of the 'fillers' they use. Having listened to the tape in the target language again to identify the target-language 'fillers', they could compare both sets of 'fillers'. They might also be given a list of other 'fillers' in the target language and asked to select possible alternatives to those used on the tape. Useful expressions could then be written on cards and hung on the ceiling so that when learners hesitate, they have only to glance upwards for support. The third time they listen to the tape, they might be asked to identify any occasion when the non-native speaker has clearly 'picked up on' an expression the hotel receptionist used, having initially used circumlocution as a way round it.
3 General practice *Circumlocution*	Learners play the party game 'Taboo' in groups of four. The game can be differentiated according to the level of the learners. Each pair competes against the other. Pairs take it in turns to pick a card on which an object is given, which they must describe to their partner so that they can guess it within an allotted time. A simple version might require them to describe the object using any words they like, or might even supply some useful words in the target language and accompanying pictures. At a higher level, it must be described without using the other three related words on the card. The game 'Just a minute', where the learner has to talk on a topic without using the word itself serves a similar function. A simpler version might allow them to use all-purpose expressions in the target language like 'thingamabob' and talk for only 30 seconds.
Keeping it simple	Two ideas from Johnstone (1989, p. 163) may be particularly useful here: • Teacher gives a short written message about a room-booking to half of the class, which is read but is then collected in. After a time delay of 15 minutes, they must pass on the message orally to their partner. Since we can only retain exact information in the working memory for a few seconds, the message will have to be reconstructed; • Learners have an urgent phone call to make but only enough money for 60 seconds (i.e. similar to the 'telegraphese' task but this time in the target language and in spontaneous speech rather than in writing or a recorded message). A further whole-class activity is a team game where the fastest team to reduce the teacher's message to 10 words wins.

Table 4.10 continued

Stage in cycle	Activity
Reviewing	Pairs listen to their original recorded conversation of the communicative task and identify how it could be improved by the use of communication strategies. They may wish to refer back to the 'bare-bones' and more sophisticated version of the task that they developed in their first language and to make a final decision on which version they will attempt, now that they have strategies at their disposal to compensate for the 'gaps'. Pairs rerecord the conversation. Each pair awards the other pair marks for the appropriate use of strategies.
4 Action planning	The final recording is marked by the teacher and returned. Learners write down a list of their own weaknesses and of useful strategies to help overcome them for future communicative tasks, e.g.: 'hesitation; to use fillers'. Teacher adds their own suggestions to the lists.
5 Focused practice and fading out the reminders	Further communicative tasks are set, both those which have been prepared in previous lessons and those which have not. Learners use the strategies identified in their action plan. Some are likely to be common to most learners. For example, to help them recombine elements from familiar topics in novel ways ('Making the most of what you have got'), Johnstone (1989, p. 155) suggests using sets of cards on which topics, functions, contexts, and details of speakers' age, gender etc., are given. Learners select cards from each set (e.g. health, complaining, beach) and must devise an appropriate conversation. Activities for 'keeping it simple' that could also be offered to the whole class include: • imagining they are newspaper reporters and turning an account of an accident into a telegram; • writing a television advert, where each word costs £1,000. Learners can be placed in pairs with a communicative task to perform with the aim of practising any other strategies identified on their particular action plan. After some time has elapsed, class is simply reminded to use communication strategies.
6 Evaluating strategy acquisition and recommencing the cycle	Learner and teacher evaluate success of action plans. In their subsequent action plans, some high-attaining learners may need to be encouraged to stretch themselves by moving away from the 'bare-bones' model. Under-confident learners may need further practice in the use of 'fillers' or turn-giving gambits.

Table 4.11 Cycle of strategy instruction: communication strategies (illus. 2)

	Arranging an outing with a friend
Stage in cycle	*Activity*
1 **Awareness-raising**	Learners are given the communicative task of arranging an outing 'cold'.
2 **Modelling: 'keeping it going'**	
'Turn-getting' and *'turn-giving'* gambits	Learners perform the task in their first language noting turn-getting and turn-giving gambits. They then listen to an audio recording in the target language to identify the language used to fulfil the 'gambits'. They might be asked to select possible alternatives from a list provided.
Topic manipulation	Learners listen to a similar discussion but between a native and a non-native speaker. They can be asked to guess from the recording the topics the speaker could and could not discuss in detail and the language used to nominate a new topic ('Have you heard that . . .?') or to avoid one ('I don't know anything about that'). They might also identify any 'filler' topics for keeping the conversation going, such as weather, etc.
3 **General practice: 'keeping it going'** *'Turn-getting'* gambits *and picking up on expressions used*	'Stop the teacher.' Teacher starts talking in the target language about a recent outing, their hobbies, etc. If they can talk uninterrupted for 30 seconds, they gain a point. If a learner can interrupt them with a turn-getting gambit, the class scores a point, e.g.: 'Talking about hobbies, I like to . . .' or 'By the way . . .' or 'Last weekend? Well, I went to . . .'. Extra points are awarded to the class for words or expressions that the interrupter has 'picked up' from the teacher. The game can be replicated by learners working in groups, where each member scores a point if they can interrupt another with an appropriate comment.
Topic manipulation and 'turn-giving' gambits	Learners work in pairs. One starts on a simple topic. When the teacher rings a bell, the other must introduce a new topic of conversation. Each learner must support the other ('How interesting'; 'I see', etc.), while their partner is talking. Edmunds (1995) suggests how support to build in some of this language could be provided in previous lessons. She sets up a simple group task and assigns each member a role, teaching them simple expressions to fulfil it e.g.: 'encourager' ('What do you think?'), 'praiser' ('Good idea'; 'Very interesting'). This allows the learner to practise inserting the necessary expressions into the conversation.

Table 4.11 continued

Stage in cycle	Activity
'Fillers' and 'turn-taking' and 'turn-giving' gambits	Groups of learners play a game called 'Make it fit'. Each member has 5 cards on which are written expressions for 'fillers', turn-taking/giving gambits. The first player starts a conversation on the topic of their choice. As soon as they or another member of the group can insert one of the expressions on their card into the conversation, they can discard it. The winner is the first to get rid of all their cards.
Reviewing	Pairs listen to their recorded conversation of the communicative task and identify how it could be improved by the use of communication strategies. Pairs rerecord the initial conversation. Each pair awards the other pair marks for the appropriate use of strategies.
4 Action planning	Final recording assessed by teacher and returned. Pupils write down a list of their own weaknesses and a list of useful strategies to help overcome them for future communicative tasks.
5 Focused practice and fading out the reminders	Further communicative tasks are set; both those which have been prepared in previous lessons and those which have not. Learners use the strategies they have identified in their action plan. After some time has elapsed, class is simply reminded to use communication strategies.
6 Evaluating strategy acquisition and recommencing the cycle	Pupil and teacher evaluate success of action plans and a new action plan is negotiated.

Strategy instruction should be integrated into everyday lessons

Holec (1996) describes the relative advantages and disadvantages of separate as opposed to integrated instruction of strategies. Separate instruction entails a course which takes place before or parallel to the language lessons. In an English secondary school context, such instruction might be labelled 'Study Skills' and be part of the 'Personal, Social and Moral Education' curriculum. However valuable this may be in allowing learners to identify useful strategies common to all subject areas, there are arguments for integrating specific strategy instruction into modern languages lessons as well. Holec (ibid., p. 99) indicates the opportunities it provides the learners to: 'draw upon, experiment with and immediately apply in his language learning what he has learnt in learning to learn'. Not only is the relevance of strategies to modern languages thus reinforced, it also provides regular opportunities for them to be proceduralised in a meaningful way. Little (1996) warns that it should not be assumed that merely 'training' students in strategy use will automatically lead to the development of their communicative competence; communicative tasks must remain at the core of their classroom experiences. He draws an analogy between the successful deployment of grammatical rules and the successful deployment of strategies, arguing that both depend on the gradual development of psychological processes, that can be facilitated but not replaced by pedagogical measures. He argues that:

> Some pedagogical traditions have devoted so much time to the explanation, illustration and memorization of grammatical rules that no time has been left to develop communicative ability; much the same danger attends the current obsession in some quarters with 'strategy training'.
>
> (Little 1996, p.26)

Little's assertion is that strategy instruction should reflect a communicative view of the nature and purpose of language learning and should promote learner autonomy. This view also relates to other assumptions underlying the model.

The purpose of strategy instruction should be made explicit to the learners

In embedded instruction, learners are presented with activities and materials designed to elicit the use of the strategies being taught but are not informed of the reasons underlying the particular approach. However, Little (1997) argues for a direct approach; consciousness raising should invite learners to engage reflectively in task planning, execution and assessment, thereby extending the range of strategic competencies they bring to the classroom and offering them control of their learning. As we argued in Chapter 2, this involvement of the learner in making choices is central to the development of autonomy. Similarly, Rubin (1992) defines 'executive control' as consisting of three processes: the setting of goals; the monitoring of performance or comprehension and of any problems that arise; and the making of decisions as to appropriate subsequent action. The taxonomy of strategies we referred to in Chapter 2 from the 1996 Council of Europe publication – *Modern Languages: Learning, Teaching and Assessment. A Common European Framework of Reference*, stresses the same central processes, grouping strategies under the categories of planning, execution, evaluation and repair (section 4.8). The steps in our cycle of 'awareness raising', 'action planning' and 'evaluation' reflect the concern, expressed in all three publications, to empower the learner by making the learning process explicit and providing them with opportunities to direct their own learning. Furthermore, O'Malley and Chamot (1990, p.153) report that the addition of such metacognitive elements has been helpful in maintaining strategy use over time and in transferring strategies to new tasks. If it is also the case that success depends not on the use of one individual strategy but on the effective management of a repertoire of strategies, then learners themselves need to be able to make conscious, informed choices.

The exact location of the action-planning step within our cycle is debatable and may depend on the nature of the strategies to be taught. In the examples we offer, action planning has come after the general-practice stage in order to expose learners to the full range of strategies available before selecting those most appropriate to their needs. In the case of the memorisation strategies, however, as some of them may be familiar already and the new ones are relatively straight-forward, action planning could precede the practice stage, particularly since the strategies are common to whatever items of vocabulary are to be learned. The decision for the learner is simply to establish which strategies will help them address their particular area of difficulty (recall of gender, spelling, etc.). In contrast, some reading strategies are more relevant than others for particular texts, and learners may need to be exposed to a range of strategies and text types, before deciding on which to focus. Similarly, learners may never have reflected before on strategies for checking written work or communication strategies and an understanding of the range of possibilities, alongside feedback on their work, may first be necessary before they are in a position to select the most appropriate personal goals.

Strategy instruction should involve collaborative learning

If learners are to reflect on what they learn and how, such negotiation will involve collaborative and project-based learning, where learners can 'share' the consciousness of their peers. As we previously discussed, in a Vygotskian model of learning, language is not an isolated, individual activity but rather an internalisation of what was originally a social activity taking place in classrooms that are themselves sociocultural communities. The steps of the cycle in which learners brainstorm together how they approached the task, or model their own preferred strategies for each other, or practise new strategies together in pairs or groups, or check each other's work, all seek to take account of this view. The action-planning step provides a further opportunity to create a shared discourse, as Donato and McCormick (1994) suggest of their portfolio project, which represented 'an attempt to create a community of language learning practice in which learners had frequent opportunity to externalize in discourse to their instructor and themselves their own learning'.

Strategy instruction should be in the target language as far as possible

If strategy instruction should be directed towards the development of communicative competence, and if it involves collaborative negotiation and reflection, then a central role must be accorded to the use of the target language if competence is to become routinised. Discussing and evaluating what is to be learned, and how, is, after all, one of the few classroom activities that requires learners to use the target language for genuinely communicative purposes. This is, however, a controversial issue, particularly with beginner classes. We have seen how checklists, such as those for memorisation strategies, can be written in the target language, provided they are accompanied by visual support. Perhaps even the action plan can be written in the target language if pupils are involved in drawing up a list of possible expressions from which to choose. With most beginner classes, however, it is likely that the awareness raising in step 1 and the evaluation in step 6 would have to be in the first language initially. The aim here is to get all the class participating and reflecting on their learning. The effort of explaining themselves in the target language may well deter all but the highest attainers from contributing to the discussion. In the long term, any disadvantages produced by not using the target language one hundred per cent of the time may be offset by an increase in pupil motivation, independence and performance. As the class begins to become familiar with the process of reflecting on their own learning, however, they can be taught gradually how to make their com-ments in the target language, especially if the language is kept simple. For example, the expression 'je trouve ça difficile' ('I find that difficult') applies equally well, not only to different school subjects (a common topic for secondary school beginners) but also to difficulties encountered in memorising vocabulary.

Strategy instruction should be geared towards the level and needs of the learners

In devising the illustrations, it was necessary to establish some notion of the level of the learners and hence to determine which strategies should be taught when. Drawing on the developmental order suggested in Chapter 2, a decision was made to direct the examples of reading and listening strategies and 'mem-orisation strategies' towards beginner learners, and 'checking written work' and 'communication strategies' to intermediate learners. It could be argued that it is possible to teach some of the more 'simple' communication strategies, or those involved in checking work, to beginner learners and some suggestions have been provided. Nevertheless, as we have seen, the 'receptive' skill areas may be more accessible than spontaneous speech or the strategies involved in checking written work.

This is not, however, to imply a simplistic solution to the problems of designing a syllabus for strategy instruction: that memorisation strategies should be taught in year one of the course; then reading and listening strategies in year two; and checking work in year three, etc. It is clear that within the skill areas, some tasks and hence the strategies that are needed are more or less demanding than others. Within listening, for example, using inferencing to discover the meaning of a particular word used in an exchange in a shop may be easier than using inferencing to determine someone's underlying attitudes from a discussion on environmental issues or following a lecture on a scientific topic. Similarly, identifying cognates is relatively straightforward but strategies involving knowl-edge of the grammar of the language to work out the meaning may be more complex. Thus some reading and listening strategies may be appropriate for year one, others may be introduced in year three and so on. This does, however, involve some serious planning to ensure progression from one year to the next.

Since the level of the learners is clearly significant, before commencing the cycle, the teacher will wish to select the strategies they particularly want the class to learn. It can be useful to observe learners while they are working to establish those that appear already familiar. The following criteria may also guide the selection process:

- those that appear to be within the grasp of the particular age group. As already indicated, it may be helpful to take into account the developmental order discussed in Chapter 2 and referred to at the end of Chapter 3 in relation to the stage of development of the three learners;
- those strategies that can be practised within the particular learning context. Learners living in the target-language community have opportunities to seek out and engage in discussions with native speakers or to watch the television in the target language that learners in a foreign-language context do not. Access to different types of reading and listening texts may vary from one context to the other and constrain choices;
- those strategies that are most readily transferable. Cognates, for example, are useful in comprehending both written and spoken texts and across a range of genres. Holding unfamiliar sounds in your head and saying them over and over again may well be an important listening strategy but is restricted to that particular skill;
- those strategies that are most readily teachable. Again, taking cognates as an example, we have seen that these are relatively straightforward to teach, whereas the communication strategy of topic manipulation is harder.

Conclusion

In this chapter, we have shown what teaching strategies might look like in practice. We have also discussed some of the theoretical justifications for strategy instruction. We have sought to give a positive picture of the use of learning strategies. However, it is obviously a complex process. In Part One of this book, we identified some of the many variables that effect strategy use: some to do with the individual learner – for example, background knowledge, proficiency level, cultural background, gender, etc.; others to do with the task itself – such as level of difficulty, language modality, etc. The interaction between the variables may also be significant. How effective strategy instruction may be for particular learners will therefore depend on:

- who they are;
- the particular strategies taught;
- how the strategies are taught: the cycle of steps adopted – most notably the opportunities offered to the learners to internalise the strategies and to make choices about the most appropriate strategies for the particular task in hand.

Clearly, there are also a whole lot of attitudinal and motivational factors involved in language learning, which may amplify or undermine the effects of strategy instruction (see Gillette 1994).

Some researchers have concluded that until further studies into the effectiveness of strategy instruction are undertaken 'a pedagogic decision of some risk has to be taken to devote teaching time to strategy training rather than language learning' (McDonough 1995, p. 83). Kellerman (1991, p.158) suggests that the risk is not worth taking, since learners already bring their existing strategic competence in L1 to the modern-languages classroom. The conclusion to this argument is that we should teach learners more language and let the strategies take care of themselves. However, the issue of whether learners' strategic competence in their first language is sufficient is highly debatable. In relation to communication strategies, we have already noted that not all learners may be aware of turn-giving strategies. Furthermore, since strategies often operate at an unconscious level, it may not be apparent that they can be transferred to a new language. The sort of strategy training we have offered has two main advantages: first, directly on the assimilation of language; second, indirectly in building up a repertoire of cognitive skills which can be employed in pedagogic and natural learning contexts. As in all applied linguistic research, it is a mistake to over-extrapolate on a few empirical studies and to make unrealistic claims on the basis of insubstantial research. Nevertheless, we believe that the strategies offered in this chapter, and the cycle involved in training learners to use them, integrate the pedagogic and linguistic processes of language learning in a way that has largely been unexplored in the methodologically prescriptive context of the secondary school modern-languages classroom. We shall return to this discussion in the concluding chapter of the book. First, however, unless what we offer here should be considered an idealisation detached from real classroom practice, we want to look at what happened when a group of teachers did work with their pupils on developing learning strategies in modern-languages lessons. This is the topic of the next chapter.

Translation of the Dutch poem

This is a translation of the Dutch poem, Figure 4.1, on p. 76.

> An apple is red,
> The sun is yellow,
> The sky is blue,
> A leaf is green,
> A cloud is white . . .
> And the earth is brown.
>
> And now would you be able to answer
> the question
>
> What colour is love?

From *Welke kleur de liefde?*, by Joan Walsh Anglund (Wageningen, Holland: Zomer and Keuning).

5 Strategy instruction in action

By becoming self-conscious, collaborative and critical about their teaching, teachers develop more power over their professional lives and are better able to create classrooms and schools that are responsive to the vision they and we have for our children's future.

(Hopkins 1993 p. 7)

For me as a classroom researcher, it has been very interesting to observe my learners keenly – to open my eyes wider than usual, trying to see exactly what learning is taking place and how it is happening. It has been exciting and also frustrating; for in the end the learning actually happens inside the learners' heads – invisible and unquantifiable. So I finish the project with more questions than I began with. Thus the project has been not only a learning experience for the pupils, but also valuable for me as their teacher.

(Fiona Lunskey, classroom teacher)

Introduction

The last two decades have seen a proliferation of studies exploring the notion of the 'teacher as researcher'. The metaphor of 'reflective practice' has had considerable influence in thinking about teacher education in Britain and the USA (see for example, Schön 1983, 1987 and Grenfell 1998b for a fuller discussion specifically in the light of modern-languages teacher education). In this chapter, we look at a group of teachers exploring their own practice and the learning of their pupils by working with strategies. Their experiences formed part of a professional development course where both the theory and practice of learning strategies were addressed. We shall consider the problems these teachers hoped strategy instruction would help them to address. We shall also examine how easy they found it to translate some of the ideas on strategy instruction set out in Chapter 4 into suitable teaching activities and materials for their particular pupils. How did the pupils respond to strategy instruction and what conclusions did the teachers reach about their future classroom practice? To what extent do their conclusions illustrate or challenge the principles of strategy instruction we have discussed?

What follows is a series of case studies of strategy instruction in action. They involve five modern-languages teachers: Angelina, Pamela, Marian, Jacqui and Fiona. The period of time they had both to implement and evaluate the strategy instruction was limited to four months. All of the teachers were working in state schools at the time of their strategy work; often in deprived areas. Each was working with a different age group, ranging from 11–16 years old, and sometimes with different sets of strategies. Two of the case studies focus on the teaching of memorisation strategies, the third and fourth on speaking strategies and the fifth on reading strategies. The methods the teachers used to evaluate their projects were broadly similar. However, a feature of the case studies is to render visible how difficult it can be to collect robust information on learners' language-learning strategies. Nevertheless, it is possible to focus on pupils' responses to the strategy work in a way which raises a number of practically based questions concerning their language learning.

The account of the case studies will describe any significant similarities and differences in the implementation of the cycle of strategy instruction and in pupils' responses. Differences in classroom organisation will also be discussed. Having described the five projects, we will attempt to draw some general conclusions, relating the teachers' practical experiences to theory, to previous research findings and to possible implications for the model of strategy instruction outlined in Chapter 4.

Case studies 1 and 2: teaching memorisation strategies

Angelina and Pamela

Angelina teaches French in an inner-city girls' secondary school in south London, where many of the pupils come from local ethnic communities. Pamela teaches in a mixed comprehensive school in Essex, the catchment area of which is largely working class. Both of them are concerned that their pupils seem unable to retain even simple items of vocabulary from one lesson to the next. Angelina comments on her year 10 (fourth year of secondary school: age 14–15 years) 'bottom set':

> such a scenario is detrimental in that the learner begins to perceive herself as a failure and may cease to attempt to learn the language. This in turn leaves the teacher struggling to manage a difficult and disaffected group of pupils.

In Pamela's case, the problems of pupils' poor retention of vocabulary was compounded by the fact that her year 9 class (third year of secondary school: age 13–14 years) study both French and German on a carousel. Here, half of the year is spent studying one language, the remaining half the other and the syllabus for each language has therefore to be covered in a very short time. Angelina hoped that by teaching her disaffected girls memorisation strategies, they might not only experience a degree of success but also recognise that there were simple tools they could use that would allow them to take control of their learning. Rather than passively accepting that they were 'no good at French', they might come to see that they could do something practical and concrete to ensure they made progress. Pamela had similar objectives but was particularly interested in the boys' response. The underachievement of boys in all subject areas, not least in language learning, is a source of current concern in Britain. She was aware that Graham and Rees's study (1995) had suggested that whereas girls may respond to failure by becoming anxious and working harder, often by rote learning, some boys attribute their lack of progress to the fact that the work seems irrelevant to them or does not meet their 'personal agenda', so that they then feel justified in 'mucking about'. She felt that this might relate to attribution theory (discussed in Chapter 4); the boys attributing their lack of achievement to fixed causes ('French is boring and a waste of time') and the girls feeling more in control of their learning and aware of some strategies. While she did not feel it was possible within the time constraints of the project to provide them with more 'say' in *what* was to be learned, she was curious to see if, at least by making explicit *how* to tackle memorising vocabulary, the boys would feel more in charge of their learning and make better progress.

The projects

Angelina's project

Angelina had little difficulty in integrating strategy instruction into her usual lessons during the spring term, since vocabulary-learning homework was a regular feature of her lessons. Following the cycle outlined in Chapter 4, she began by giving the pupils a test 'cold' and then brainstorming the strategies they used and encouraging them to model for each other the strategies that worked for them. She modelled other strategies herself that they were not yet using; 'translating' the strategies identified by O'Malley and Chamot (1990) into words that her pupils could readily understand and provide examples for. As a result, she produced the checklist illustrated in Figure 4.6 in Chapter 4 (see p. 91), which pupils had to tick for the next two learning homeworks. Lessons proceeded as usual but she reduced the number of reminders for the following three weeks of learning homeworks, by withdrawing the checklist. Alongside the strategy instruction, Angelina found other simple ways of allowing pupils some 'say' in the lessons; by inviting them to suggest the items of vocabulary to be learned, for example. Her desire to involve them had, however, to be reconciled with her own need to collect reliable information. While taking account of pupils' suggestions, she had also to ensure comparability of difficulty across the tests, considering factors such as cognates, length, number of syllables, etc. Other activities aimed at fostering some independence included negotiating a marking system for the tests with the students (1 mark for the correct word, 1 for accurate spelling, 1 for correct

	UTILISE	N'UTILISE PLUS	RAISONS:
NOM: Louisa CLASSE: DATE:			
Stratégies pour apprendre les mots et phrases.			
Essayez ces stratégies. Cochez les stratégies que vous avez essayées. Dites pourquoi.			
1 Je répète les mots ou phrases	✔		*ça m'a aidée*
2 Je répète rythmiquement		✔	*c'est nul*
3 J'utilise mon cahier et mon index	✔		*c'est facile*
4 Je fais des mind-maps		✔	*c'est ennuyeux*
5 Je mets des étiquettes		✔	*c'est ennuyeux*
6 J'écris le français et l'anglais	✔		*c'est facile*
7 Je me demande/je demande à une copine/Je demande à mon prof . . .dans cet ordre	✔		*c'est facile*
8 Je travaille (tranquillement!) avec une amie		✔	*trop difficile*
9 Je m'organise bien pour travailler		✔	*c'est nul*
10 Je m'enregistre sur une cassette		✔	*c'est ennuyeux*
11 J'écoute la cassette		✔	*c'est nul*
12 Je lis en silence	✔		*c'est facile*
13 Je lis a haute voix		✔	*c'est ennuyeux*

Figure 5.1 Pupils' checklist for evaluating memorisation strategies

gender, etc.) and providing spaces in the lessons, where they could work together to use the strategies to learn vocabulary and give each other 'mini-tests'.

At the end of the term, she reissued the checklist and asked pupils to comment on the reasons they had or had not used the strategies, offering them a choice of possible expressions in the target language.

In order to establish the level of retention of the strategies, five weeks after the end of the project, pupils completed a questionnaire, noting which strategies they were still using (Figure 5.1). Since Angelina wanted to probe in more depth pupils' responses to strategy instruction, she also interviewed a representative sample of pupils with a range of attainment levels and personal characteristics such as confidence and motivation. The interviews were recorded and transcribed. Pupils were asked if they had used strategies before the strategy instruction; which ones they were continuing to use; which they had rejected and why; and whether they had found the strategy instruction helpful. Angelina was aware, however, that terms such as 'level of attainment' and 'personality' are far from unproblematic and that, however hard she tried, her assessment of pupils was bound to remain highly subjective. Clearly, there were limitations concerning the information she was able to collect on her pupils. They might try to produce the right answers, simply to please her. Less articulate pupils might have difficulty in making explicit the strategies they used. Nevertheless, she hoped that by using a range of techniques to evaluate her project, she would gain some insight into her pupils' responses.

Pamela's project

Pamela implemented the cycle of strategy instruction for memorisation strategies in a similar way to Angelina. Like her, she set up opportunities for pupils to work in pairs. Two minor differences are, however, worth noting. First, she produced a bar chart showing each pupil's test results on a weekly basis (see Figure 5.2). These were displayed on parents' evening.

Second, Pamela introduced the strategies more gradually. For example, it was not until the third week that she modelled word association. She also took note of problems that pupils continued to experience and introduced relevant strategies. For example, since recalling the gender of words was often a difficulty, she suggested the use of visual support; although the dangers of stereotyping were discussed, she followed their proposal that 'cold' masculine words should be written with blue icicles and 'warm' feminine words in red flames. These visuals were displayed in the designated 'strategy corner' which she had set up in the classroom.

The pupils' responses

Both teachers noted an improvement in the vocabulary test scores following strategy instruction; although in both cases, the most dramatic improvement was the test directly following the brainstorming session. Pamela surmises that

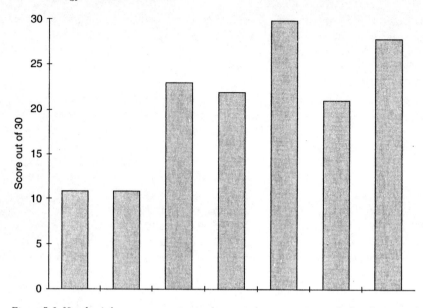

Figure 5.2 Kandice's last seven test scores (strategy instruction started after the second test)

possible reasons for the lack of consistent progress were that the 'novelty' value may have diminished and also, perhaps, because of her own unavoidable absence for a number of the later lessons: 'taking away the teacher is like fading the reminders, and in this case it occurred too early in the learning process'. In most tests, the boys scored below the class average and the girls above it. The girls were also more consistent in terms of individual improvement. At interview with the two boys, Joe's responses to strategy instruction appeared negative; trying out new strategies 'didn't appeal to me' and 'I haven't tried'. However, given that one month later he had transferred two strategies to the task of learning grammatical rules and had scored well on the subsequent test, Pamela was uncertain whether he was reluctant to try anything new or whether he was not prepared to admit in front of Mark, his friend, that he was in fact exploring new strategies. Recognising the issue of peer pressure during interview, she then interviewed Mark alone.

Angelina was particularly pleased to see that Karen, who had struggled with language learning throughout her time in school, managed to excel in the tests, even after the reminders were faded. Karen commented during the interview that she had started to work with her friends to learn the new vocabulary. Indeed, in analysing the checklists to establish the most popular strategies, Angelina and Pamela noted that although 'basic' mechanical strategies, such as repetition and copying the words out seemed to be the most widely used, the next most popular were interactive strategies. Table 5.1 offers a run down of the strategies used by the pupils in Angelina's class.

Table 5.1 Analysis of checklists

Strategy	No of mentions
Repetition	17
Writing French and English	16
Read in silence	14
Read aloud	13
Using exercise book and index	10
Work with a friend	10
Organising work	9
Asking self/friend/teacher	8
Labelling	4
Repetition with a rhythm	1
Mind-maps	0
Recording oneself	0
Listening to tape	0

Notes:
Table shows usage of strategies by all pupils in descending order
Two pupils did not complete.

Some pupils made use of word association; one remembered the word 'montre' because 'it shows the time'. In terms of 'visual association', another pupil thought of keys (*clés*) made of clay. It appeared from the interviews that pupils were reluctant to adopt the more time-consuming strategies such as recording themselves and drawing mind-maps. The exception was 'look–cover–test–check' in Pamela's school, and she surmises that this was because they were encouraged to use this strategy in other subject areas. She notes that pupils may need more explanation of what is involved in developing a photographic memory; 'look at the page, close your eyes and try to see it in your mind, look at the page again and spot what you forgot'. The need to unpack what is involved in a strategy has already been discussed in Chapter 4 in relation to 'checking written work' or 'keeping it simple'.

Pamela observed that very few pupils used a combination of strategies to learn a word, such as association for its gender and gapped letters to practise spelling it accurately. Her observation that: 'the links between the particular problems they are experiencing and the strategies that will help them need to be made explicit' reinforces the value of the action plan, described in Chapter 4.

About three quarters of Angelina's pupils had extended the range of strategies they used by the end of the spring term. Seventy per cent of the pupils were still using two or more new strategies at the end of the project, when they completed the questionnaire (see Figure 5.3). She was interested to note that in contrast to the findings of some of the research studies, willingness to try out new strategies did not seem to be limited to high attainers. From Table 5.2, she noted that whereas pupil G, a proficient pupil, appeared to have neither tried nor adopted

Table 5.2 Analysis of strategies checklist

Pupil	Total no. of strategies used (out of 10)	New strategies tried	New strategies adopted at end of project (March)
A	4	2	2
B	7	3	3
C	5	4	4
D	2	2	0
E	5	0	0
F	7	4	4
G	5	0	0
H	7	5	5
I	5	0	0
J	5	1	1
K	4	2	2
L	6	4	4
M	–	–	–
N	7	4	3
O	5	3	3
P	8	7	1
Q	7	4	3
R	–	–	–
S	6	4	4
T	7	3	3

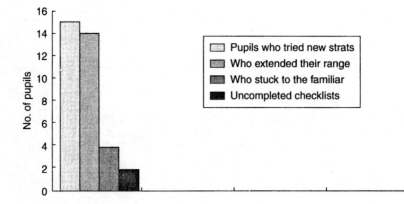

Figure 5.3 Analysis of the strategies checklist

any new strategies, pupils F and L, low attainers, had adopted four new strategies by the end of the project. Similarly, Pamela found that attainment levels did not always determine whether a pupil was willing to try out new strategies and 'personality' seemed to be an important factor: 'If we compare Kandice with Emma, both "high attainers" within the group, Kandice who is a "stronger" personality is more willing to take risks than Emma who is "reserved"'. Emma explained during the interview that she had found that the familiar strategy 'look–cover–test–check' had worked well for her and was reluctant to adopt others, especially as when she did, her test results dropped. Kandice, on the other hand, tried out a range of strategies and appeared from the interview to be aware which strategies would be most useful for her to acquire. She had no difficulties in remembering the meaning of a word, so she did not undertake associated strategies, like the mind map. Recognising that accuracy was a weakness, she chose to adopt strategies like writing out the words and using colour-coding for gender. She transferred the latter strategy across from the learning of French to the learning of German: 'they do "die, das and der", so I do green, red and blue . . . so that helps'.

Some of the benefits of the focus on strategies emerged during the interviews, with one of Angelina's pupils commenting that: 'we're working together more and just spending more time'. The problems of pupils' ability and willingness to articulate how they are learning was also evident. For example, Angelina had seen from her notes that pupil K had used the relatively complex strategy of word association, linking 'vendeur' (salesperson) to a vending machine and 'pompier' (fire officer) to someone pumping water onto a fire but she did not report using the strategy.

Pamela found that her pupil interviews offered her some insight into the social problems that restrict the possibility for some pupils to adopt certain strategies and highlighted the role peer support can play in enhancing pupils' learning. A number of pupils reported that trouble at home made it difficult to concentrate on homework and Kandice's family were not willing to test her on her vocabulary. Joanna scored highly in her tests when working with a friend but her scores fell as soon as they had quarrelled. Pamela subsequently suggested that Joanna and Kandice should do their learning homework together.

Although action planning was not included in her cycle of strategy instruction, Pamela took advantage of the interviews to move pupils forward in their learning. For example, she felt that Mark was ready to move on to more 'adventurous' strategies and he welcomed her suggestion to use colour-coding to recall the gender of words. By the end of the interview with Joanna, she noted that she seemed: 'to accept the idea that her difficulties may have been due to a lack of effective strategies rather than a lack of attainment'.

Referring back to her initial aim to boost pupils' motivation by giving them more control of their learning, Angelina comments:

> The link between strategy use, progress and motivation is hard to quantify
> . . . Field notes, interviews and observation demonstrate a general increase in

confidence and a greater willingness to attempt more difficult tasks. Pupils F and K no longer 'feel bad'. Charlene says: 'it works, I understand what the work is about . . .' Alongside this increased motivation has come increased cooperation and a decrease in dependence on the teacher. In a lesson where pupils were observed learning before a test, only two of them chose to work alone. The others worked in pairs and there was one group of five pupils testing each other and spelling words orally using the target language. In a class where a number of pupils have behavioural difficulties, it is quite an achievement for them to be responsible enough to dictate how they learn and with whom and to use their time effectively without input from the teacher.

Future directions

What then do Angelina and Pamela see as the next step forward in their schools? The time constraints of their projects, completed over a 4-month period, emerge as problematic, as they believe that it was artificial to fade out the reminders so quickly. Low attainers require more practice and reinforcement, such as posters on the wall, written comments in their books etc. Pamela also notes that some of them needed considerable persuasion to adopt new strategies. She observes that, although the test results were a motivating factor for many pupils, it may be important to convince anxious learners such as Emma, to persist with new strategies even if at first they do not yield results. Angelina points out that not just low attainers but high attainers too can benefit from strategy instruction. She describes how one pupil from a 'top set' class observed her 'bottom set' pupils revising for a test during break-time and commented 'why can't we do that?' Pamela too is keen to extend strategy instruction to other classes but believes that it should commence from year 7 (first year of secondary school: aged 11–12 years). By the end of the project, both teachers were convinced that learning strategies are relevant across the curriculum but that teachers of all subjects need to collaborate in order to provide coherent and systematic support for their development.

Case studies 3 and 4: speaking skills and memorisation strategies

Marian and Jacqui

Although in Marian's classroom, the focus is also on memorisation strategies, there are a number of features which make it different from Angelina and Pamela's undertakings. At the time of the project, Marian was an advisory teacher for a south London borough. She had been invited to help one of the teachers in the school who wanted to: 'fight her propensity to control everything that was going on in the classroom'. Strategy instruction formed part of a wider project designed to shift control and management of learning from the teacher to the learners. From her previous experiences in local schools, Marian commented: 'What has been obvious to me in many of these group-work situations is that, while the more proficient learners appear to flourish and are clearly empowered, the less successful learner seems to flounder, often loses heart and sometimes drops out of the process altogether'. She refers to similar concerns about the lack of sufficient 'scaffolding' in lessons (see Grenfell and Harris 1993). A further observation she had made was about the failure of pupils to engage in any real depth in the group-speaking tasks. Whereas they were prepared to use dictionaries in reading and writing tasks, or to rewind the tape in listening tasks, the speaking tasks were often completed as rapidly as possible, with the minimum amount of effort. The class she was due to work with was a year 11 (fifth year of secondary schools: aged 15–16 years) in a girls' school in south-east London. They had recently completed their 'mock' GCSE examination: a trial run, or rehearsal of the real thing. The results, particularly for the speaking test, were disappointing and the girls were demoralised and unmotivated. Marian, therefore, was faced with a dilemma. Although they were unlikely to take speaking tasks in group work seriously, they were also likely to resist whole-class teaching, because of their increased self-consciousness and: 'a sense of frustration at apparently remaining as dependent on their teachers at this latter stage of language learning as they were in the initial stages'. She sought to tackle the problem in three ways: first, by choosing a topic which she thought would engage the pupils' interest; second, by insisting that there should be a long-term purpose to the group work in the form of an oral presentation to the rest of the class; and third, by teaching the pupils memorisation strategies. Recognising that memorising vocabulary is one of the first things pupils need to be able to do in order to begin to generate their own utterances, she decided to focus on these strategies during strategy instruction in the hope that the pupils' improved retention of language would lead to a greater confidence and fluency in speaking the language.

Like Marian, Jacqui was concerned to develop independent learning, but in her case it was primarily in response to the question of enhancing the effectiveness of mixed ability teaching. Pupils at her small, rural community school are not streamed according to attainment and any class contains pupils who may achieve the highest marks in the GCSE examination and those who may not even pass it. The aims of her school include: 'to promote a caring community in which each member feels equally valued and respected' and 'to encourage the idea of learning as a life-long process'. Jacqui believed that allowing pupils to work at their own pace and encouraging them to take responsibility for their progress was essential in meeting these aims. Prior to commencing the project, she had already established a programme for her year 9 (aged 13–14) German class designed to develop independent learning. For each unit of the textbook, she had provided a sheet of tasks from the book to be completed, a list of useful vocabulary and a set of answer cards. Initial observations had proved promising. Pupils were all keen, used equipment appropriately and were able to get on with their tasks, even if the class teacher was unavoidably late or absent. She was concerned, however, about the results of the tests that took place after every five units. While marks in listening and reading were high, pupils did not appear to be spending enough time on the speaking tasks and English remained the dominant language for classroom exchanges. Jacqui felt that although she had set up opportunities for pupils to have some 'say', however limited, in what and how to learn, they were failing to exploit them, perhaps because they lacked the necessary strategies. She concluded that:

> the teacher must therefore consider very carefully exactly which skills, information and training pupils will need in order to take advantage of the choices and responsibility they are to be given. The skills needed for developing productive use of the language appeared to be missing with my year 9 class and my task was to find ways of bringing them to the fore.

The projects

Marian's project

Marian was aware that it would have been unrealistic to expect pupils who were used to a teacher-dominated, whole-class approach to teaching to take complete responsibility for their learning. So, while they would be offered some limited choice as to how and when they would tackle some of the materials, the language content would be determined by the regular class teacher. Marian devised a number of tasks for the pupils to complete over a 6-week period on the topic, 'Protecting the Environment and Saving Endangered Species'. She also devised a planning sheet and an activities checklist (Figures 5.4 and 5.5) to help them plan and monitor their work. They were to work in groups of 2 or 3 on the materials with a view to preparing an oral presentation in the form of a poem, song, game or prose exposition on one aspect of the theme in the final week of the project. The pupils therefore had some choice in determining the learning outcomes.

The cycle of strategy instruction used to teach the memorisation strategies was similar to that used by Angelina and Pamela. There were two features particular to Marian's lessons, over and above the fact that pupils were engaged on a project with clearly defined long-term aims. First, she did not set regular vocabulary tests, since the main objectives of the 'environment project' were to develop pupils' general confidence and motivation in speaking and to allow them to work in groups throughout the lesson. She simply asked pupils to use the strategy checklist whenever they tackled the speaking tasks in the pack of environment materials. Second, Marian wanted to explore the relationship between pupils' metacognitive strategies (their general approach to planning and evaluating the tasks), their willingness to adopt new strategies, and the range of strategies they actually used. One month after the project had been completed, the pupils completed a questionnaire based on a cognitive acceleration model used by the borough advisory team, of which she was a member (Figure 5.6 on pages 124 and 125). In retrospect, she felt it would have been helpful to relate the questions more closely to the metacognitive strategies identified by O'Malley and Chamot (1988). She also found that, as with many numerical evaluations, the girls tended to circle the 'middle' statements. Nevertheless, it did allow her to use polygramme analysis to compare in graphic

Écrivez dans les cases les activités que vous allez faire chaque leçon *et pour les devoirs*			
semaine	*mercredi*	*vendredi*	*devoirs*
1			
2			
3			
4			
5			
6	Vacances de février		

Figure 5.4 Projet sur l'environnement: planning

L'environnement			
Activité	*commencé*	*fini*	*opinions*
1			
2			
3			
4			
5			
6			
7			
8			
9			
10			
11			
12			
13			
14			
présentation			

Figure 5.5 L'environnement

form the information drawn from the questionnaire, the memorisation check-lists, and her interviews with five pupils, representing a range of attainment levels and 'personality'. Examples of the polygramme analysis are illustrated in Figures 5.8 and 5.9, pp. 128–29.

The pupils' responses

Given the time constraints of the project, Marian understandably found it difficult to monitor pupils' acquisition of memorisation strategies, compare it to their metacognitive strategies and also conduct a systematic assessment of the development of their speaking skills. She was forced in the end to rely on her own and the classroom teacher's judgements and comments pupils made about their progress during the interview. She observed that: 'it is difficult to unpick whether improvements in retention, confidence and motivation which we felt did occur, were born out of the strategy training (the increased awareness of how to learn) or whether they happened as a result of the opportunity to make choices as to what and how they learned'.

Pupils' responses to the strategy instruction in memorisation strategies were somewhat easier to explore. Marian's pupils were similar to Pamela's and Angelina's in that they appeared to prefer more basic strategies, such as repetition. There was again a marked preference for strategies that involved working collaboratively. The extract from her project notes given below provides a lively illustration of its value.

> This lesson was devoted to the pupils practising their presentations, in preparation for the next lesson. Debbie and Charlotte are working from the OHP acetates they have prepared together. Charlotte has written out a poem on protecting the environment and Debbie has illustrated it with pictures. Charlotte is explaining the tune she has set the refrain in the poem to. Charlotte proposes that they take it in turns to read the phrases and they should both sing the refrain. She suggests they begin practising. They do this four times. They are both relaxed and smiling and clearly listening to each other. Neither however makes any comment on the other's pronunciation. Charlotte suggests they now recite the poem without the text, just using the visuals as clues. Debbie gets stuck and says she needs to see the text again. She reads her lines five times, Charlotte nodding encouragement. Debbie indicates she is ready to start again and recites her part correctly but some-what hesitantly. Charlotte says hers more confidently. Debbie is left with the last line to recite and again experiences difficulty, returning to the text. Charlotte mouths the words to her friend. They reach the end of the poem and Charlotte suggests they go through the process again. They do this three times. Charlotte explains how she thinks they should perform their presentation. Debbie has prepared a further visual with the slogan 'Sauvez l'environnement' and suggests they should place it on the OHP, when they have finished the poem and finish off their performance by both saying it

Name	Class 11A		Date 22/3/95		

Discuss the following questions with a partner and give yourself a score by ringing an appropriate answer to each question

		1	2	3	4
Attitude	How did I approach each task?	with no interest	with some interest	positively	enthusiastically
Confidence	Was I confident in tackling each task?	very unsure of myself	unsure of myself	confident	very confident
Style	Did I take time to stop and think?	none at all	not enough	sufficient	a great deal
Recognising	Did I know what to do each time?	with great difficulty	with some difficulty	easily	very easily
Defining	Did I know where to start each time?	with great difficulty	with some difficulty	easily	very easily
Planning	Did I use a useful plan each time?	inadequately	needed improvement	adequately	very successfully
Monitoring	Did I understand why I did well or not?	never	rarely	occasionally	frequently
Evaluating	Did I change my approach to tasks?	not at all	a little	to a large extent	fully
Communicating	Did I explain my ideas to others?	not at all	a little	to a large extent	fully
Skills/ knowledge	How much new language and ideas have I learnt	none	a little	some	a lot
Transferring	How much have I learnt that helps my French?	nothing at all	very little	quite a lot	a great deal
Generalising	How much have I learnt that helps other subjects?	nothing at all	very little	quite a lot	a great deal

What I liked about the project	What I disliked about the project
Being able to work at my own pace and do what I wanted to do (the interesting worksheets)	Doing class speaking work with the OHP

What could be improved	Other comments
More interesting work sheets or a variety of different kinds	I didn't like the project at first but once I'd done the work I wanted to do it made me feel like I'd achieved something so I wanted to do more for once. It actually stopped me from falling asleep in French. I think they should do more projects like it.

Figure 5.6 Student questionnaire (1)

loudly. This is the first time Debbie has initiated a suggestion regarding their presentation. Charlotte smiles and nods. They go through the presentation six times. It is now quite fluent and their performance is starting to look very confident.

One cannot help but wonder if Debbie would have been willing to practise the poem so many times had she been on her own.

The use of mind-mapping as a learning strategy for memorisation appeared to be more common than in the other two case studies, since six pupils reported using it. Although these pupils were among the higher attainers, Marian felt that the fact that mind-mapping is promoted in the Humanities department may also be significant. The popularity of the already familiar 'look–cover–test–check' has already been noted in Pamela's school.

About three-quarters of the 20 pupils were prepared to try out new strategies. Sixty-four per cent of these extended their range of strategy use, but 36 per cent chose ultimately to remain with the strategies they were already using. Again, the pupils who were unwilling to adopt new strategies did not all fit into the category of unsuccessful learners. The polygramme analysis on pages 128–129 appeared to support Marian's view of the complexity of considerations that may effect pupils' responses to strategy instruction. She notes of pupil B that she appeared to have a good level of metacognitive skills and that: 'she is quite a proficient student and is able to articulate why she does or does not use specific strategies. Her reluctance to adopt new strategies may be related more to the fact that she already feels confident as a learner'. Of mind maps, for example, the pupil said: 'Well, I write down words as well, mind maps are just set out in a different way. I find it a bit time-consuming, wondering where to put what'. In contrast, pupil C

Name		Class 11H		Date 22/3/95	

Discuss the following questions with a partner and give yourself a score by ringing an appropriate answer to each question		**1**	**2**	**3**	**4**
Attitude	How did I approach each task?	with no interest	with some interest	(positively)	enthusiastically
Confidence	Was I confident in tackling each task?	very unsure of myself	unsure of myself	(confident)	very confident
Style	Did I take time to stop and think?	none at all	(not enough)	sufficient	a great deal
Recognising	Did I know what to do each time?	with great difficulty	(with some difficulty)	easily	very easily
Defining	Did I know where to start each time?	with great difficulty	with some difficulty	(easily)	very easily
Planning	Did I use a useful plan each time?	inadequately	(needed improvement)	adequately	very successfully
Monitoring	Did I understand why I did well or not?	never	rarely	(occasionally)	frequently
Evaluating	Did I change my approach to tasks?	not at all	(a little)	to a large extent	fully
Communicating	Did I explain my ideas to others?	not at all	(a little)	to a large extent	fully
Skills/ knowledge	How much new language and ideas have I learnt	none	(a little)	some	a lot
Transferring	How much have I learnt that helps my French?	nothing at all	very little	(quite a lot)	a great deal
Generalising	How much have I learnt that helps other subjects?	nothing at all	(very little)	quite a lot	a great deal

What I liked about the project	What I disliked about the project
This was interesting and the activities were fun to do.	It was too much work, and it piled up pretty fast!

What could be improved	Other comments
Maybe not so many worksheets every lesson.	All in all, this was good and fun, the presentations were the best part as I gained confidence from this.

Figure 5.7 Student questionnaire (2)

was lacking in confidence and was one of two pupils who insisted on working alone. Her initial response to the project was negative but gradually the creative and independent aspect of it motivated her: 'it was nice to learn about the animals, and to be able to change, like, my poem, the thing about the rubbish bin eating all the rubbish, and to change it, like, to some girl saving all the animals'. Although her metacognitive strategies appeared from the questionnaire to be weaker than pupil B's and she was a less successful learner, she was ultimately more willing to adopt new strategies.

Jacqui's project

Jacqui's project was an ambitious one. In order to improve pupils' speaking skills, she set herself three targets:

- to teach memorisation strategies;
- to teach pupils activities that they could do together in their groups to improve their speaking skills;
- to teach the class some of the communication strategies they needed to use German for classroom interaction.

The intention was to mount a 'three-pronged attack', with each area feeding into the development of the other. She found that there was no one single source of reference for speaking skills but managed to draw on the list of strategies from O'Malley and Chamot (1990) and Rubin (1981) to produce the lists in Figures 5.10–5.12 on pages 130–132. As in the other case studies, she had to 'translate' the strategies into terms the pupils could understand.

At the same time as introducing the new strategies, Jacqui also decided to modify her usual classroom organisation by introducing some whole-class oral

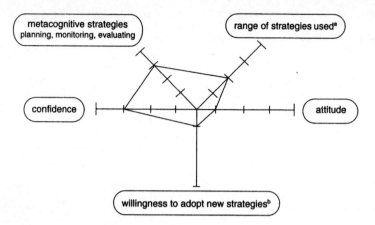

Figure 5.8   Polygramme analysis of individual pupils (pupil B)

Notes

a   The points on the line represent the number of strategies the pupil *claimed she used* as follows:

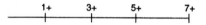

b   The points on the line represent the following:

practice into each lesson, along with regular vocabulary tests to reinforce the importance of learning homeworks. Both she and her pupils therefore needed to adapt to a number of changes. It is not surprising, therefore, that she found that she did not have time to systematically follow the cycle of strategy instruction for each of the three areas she had identified. Instead, she introduced the strategy lists to the class in the form of large posters for the classroom walls, along with a checklist for each individual pupil. Pupils were asked to choose one new strategy a week from any of the three areas and record it on their checklist. She rewarded pupils for using German in the classroom by giving them red stickers. At the end of the project, Jacqui's pupils completed a questionnaire about their learning experiences.

Like Marian, Jacqui found it hard to evaluate systematically whether pupils' speaking had improved during the time spent on the project. Nevertheless, her observations in class suggested that pupils made good use of 'Wie sagt man auf Deutsch?' ('How do you say in German?', which was written on a large poster), and that pupils admonished each other 'auf Deutsch' but mainly only when she was near them. Early on in the project, she noticed one boy in an enthusiastic group asking in English but with a German accent 'Vy don't vee . . .?' ('Why

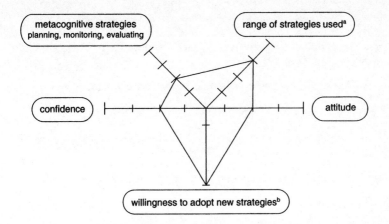

Figure 5.9 Polygramme analysis of individual pupils (pupil C)

Notes

a The points on the line represent the number of strategies the pupil *claimed she used* as follows:

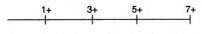

b The points on the line represent the following:

don't we . . .?').She points out that however amusing the question may sound, his attempt to at least sound German was accepted by the others in the group quite seriously. The same group appeared to latch onto the word 'Schade' (What a pity/shame), using it to comment on almost every classroom occurrence. She relates this to Wong Fillmore's (1979) 'Give the impression, with a few well-chosen words, that you speak the language' and 'Make the most of what you've got'. Otherwise, English tended largely to dominate their conversations and pupils continued to pay less attention to completing the speaking activities.

The questionnaire supported her impressions. Eighty-three per cent admitted that they were still spending less time on speaking activities than any other skill and 43 per cent said that they had not used any of the strategies at all. Although 52 per cent said that they found the posters 'quite useful', their comments point towards the need for a more systematic focus: 'we didn't look at them very carefully and sometimes forgot to use them', 'I forgot most of it that I did look at', and 'we didn't always have enough time to incorporate new ideas or games'. Jacqui was interested to see that many of these comments came from high attainers.

In terms of the vocabulary tests, there was some overall improvement. In week

---

To improve our memory for new words we can:

- Before we start learning new words, make sure we have listened to them and know the pronunciation

- Repeat them over and over either to ourselves or out loud.

- Remember them to a rhythm or tune or rap (make one up).

- Test ourselves by covering up our lists of words and trying to remember them – keep doing it every day until successful.

- Test each other (quick mini-tests), retest next day if unsuccessful.

- Play word games, e.g. Hangman – or invent new games.

- Play guessing games or Lotto.

- Write the words on pieces of paper or card and play memory and matching games like 'Pairs'.

- Use a picture or mental image to remember a word (e.g. *Rathaus* = town hall – imagine a town hall with rats running out of the front door).

- Remember 'sets' of words (e.g. days, months, etc.) make 'spidergram' notes.

- Associate new words with others you already know, or find similarities with English words (e.g. *Fussball*).

- Look out for patterns that you can remember (e.g. *Ich spiele, ich esse, ich trinke*, all end with 'e').

- Copy words out several times while concentrating hard on them.

- Record the words on a cassette – listen, then pause it and repeat the words. Rewind – replay – repeat – keep going until we're confident we have memorised the new vocabulary.

Figure 5.10 Checklist of strategies for memorising new words

1, the average mark was 6.66 and in week 4 it was 7.85. She found it useful to discuss quietly their progress on the tests with individual pupils, during group work time. For one pupil with moderate learning difficulties, for example, she suggested some strategies that she could try and set her a personal target. Her marks improved quite dramatically. Like Pamela's interviews, these one-to-one discussions appear to be fruitful.

To improve our SPEAKING we can:

- Invent and play group games with flashcards.
- Repeat new words out loud lots of times until we can remember them and say them confidently.
- Test each other's speaking or ask Frau Footman to test us:
- Give marks

$$0 \quad = \quad \ddot{\frown}$$

$$1 \quad = \quad \ddot{-}$$

$$2 \quad = \quad \ddot{\smile}$$

- Do listening work on a new topic before speaking.
- Use a cassette recording to help us get our pronunciation right (listen to the cassette then pause it and repeat the last word or phrase).
- Talk German out loud with myself using a mirror at home. Be confident, not shy about speaking.
- Read cartoon stories or plays out loud in our group. Keep practising lots of times until it sounds fairly fluent. (To do this you have to make sure you know what the words mean first.)
- When working with the 'Partnerarbeit' dialogues in the book, invent a group challenge, for example:
  - who can change the dialogue in the book to make the largest number of slightly different dialogues;
  - set a minimum time (e.g. 5 mins) to keep going, repeating but slightly changing the dialogue each time;
  - do the dialogues with the book shut, then change and/or repeat them.
- Invent and play repeatedly any sort of game that involves **speaking German.**
- Speak **German** to each other and Frau Footman **as much as possible.**

Figure 5.11 Checklist of strategies for improving speaking in groups

Future directions

Marian admits that: 'when I embarked on this project, my expectation was that the vast majority of pupils in the group would see the light and adopt new strategies'. She was therefore surprised at the resistance to change. Apart from issues such as confidence and 'personality', like the two previous teachers, she concluded that a major factor contributing to their resistance was the lack of time devoted to discussion and practice in the early stages of the cycle. Both she and Jacqui felt that more time would have allowed them to convince the

> ### To help me cope with using ONLY GERMAN to communicate in the classroom I can:

- Use expressions, mime and gestures.
- Each week, learn by heart one or two of the phrases in speech bubbles around the classroom.
- Make sure I know the phrases to use when playing a game so I **always** say things like 'your turn', 'don't cheat' and 'X has won' in German.
- Ask Frau Footman how to say something I don't know, then make a note of it so I can use it again in the future. (Wie sagt man auf Deutsch . . .?)
- Keep conversations going at all cost, even if this means pointing or miming or mixing in the odd word or two of English.
- Not be shy and always try to have a go. (We all know some things sound funny sometimes but it is unkind to make fun of other people's efforts or put them off speaking – the most important thing is for people to keep trying and experimenting – we learn things by practising and repeating.)
- Use conversation 'fillers'.

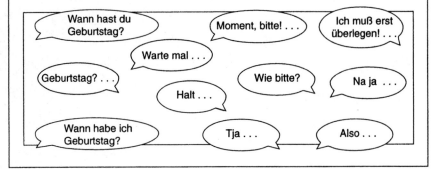

Figure 5.12 Checklist of communication strategies for speaking exclusively in the target language

successful learners not to become too complacent and the less successful to develop the confidence needed to embark on exploring new strategies. It would also have permitted Marian to explain the rationale behind certain strategies, so that perhaps pupil B would have realised that, although sometimes appearing superficially similar, strategies like copying out or mind-mapping fulfil different functions. Marian suggests a differentiated approach to the fading out of reminders; less proficient learners should be allowed more time to practise the strategies, and perhaps directed to use certain strategies appropriate to the language task, before being free to make the choices themselves. Jacqui felt that her pupils' resistance to adopting new strategies was due to: 'there being too much to focus on' and that a smaller number of strategies should have been targeted and taught through the cycle of strategy instruction.

Like Pamela, Marian believes that strategy instruction should be integrated into the language-learning curriculum from the outset. She felt that some of the year 11 pupils, who were about to leave school anyway, may have been too set in their ways to change their learning styles. Younger pupils may well be more receptive and strategy instruction should be built into the scheme of work and reviewed regularly. She raises a new issue, as she believes that if pupils are to value strategy instruction, its profile needs to be raised. She suggests not only including pupils' development of strategies in reports to parents but also ensuring that it forms part of pupils' self-assessment. This seems to lend further support to the notion that the action planning and the reviewing process play an essential part in strategy development.

A further issue raised by Jacqui concerns the use of the mother tongue and relates to the earlier discussion in Chapter 4. She concludes that certain aspects of organising the autonomous classroom, of engaging pupils in strategy instruction and of responding to individual pupils' needs are best accomplished through the judicious use of English.

Our next case study explores a new skill area: reading.

Case study 5: reading strategies

Fiona

Fiona teaches in a large, mixed comprehensive school in south-west London, the catchment area of which includes both middle- and working-class pupils. Her concern was to offer her year 7 German class an initial step towards independent learning. She felt that the large, mixed ability, beginner classes in her school were mainly kept 'on-task' by very lively teacher-centred lessons, packed with songs and games. In her view, too little time was devoted to quiet periods of independent reading, where pupils could choose what to read and could work at their own pace. She knew, however, that some of her pupils lacked the strategies they needed to be able to tackle a text without constant teacher support. Although the class included pupils like Emma, who read Dickens's novels during the registration period, other pupils had reading ages well below their chronological age and lacked reading strategies even in their mother tongue. Aware of the importance of: 'the extent to which the interactant sees the material being processed as having "personal significance"' (see Little *et al.* 1989), she was keen to offer pupils a choice of books from a well-known published reading scheme containing fictional stories.

The project

Fiona started by examining some of the existing strategy taxonomies with a view to identifying those strategies that would be comprehensible concepts for 11–12 year olds and also reasonably easy to model and teach. She had some difficulty in integrating the cycle of strategy instruction into the departmental scheme of

Reading books or articles in German

Now you have read a short story in German for fun, answer these questions about how you got on.

1 Do you think you knew a lot of the words in the text already?

I knew more words that I didn't know but I had to check the back for some phrases.

2 Did you skip over words you didn't know, and understand the general meaning of the sentences anyway?

I tried to take the main words from the sentences and find out the meaning of it, but sometimes I had to look up smaller words.

3 Did you guess some new words, because they looked like English words?

Yes, whenever I see a German word I read it through to see if it sounds like an english word then I put the word that I think it is in the sentence and see if it makes sense.

4 Did you use the pictures beside the text to help you understand what was happening in the story?

Yes, quite a lot, I could see who was talking so I didn't have to spend ages working out which character was speaking.

5 Do you think the title gave you a clue about what would happen in the story?

Not really, it just told me that there was a 'super' character in the story, I knew that it would be about saving people.

6 Did you use the word-list at the back of the booklet, or a dictionary to find out the meanings of some words?

Yes, I needed to work out some phrases and long words.

7 Did you ask a teacher to explain the meaning of some words or sentences to you?

No, those that I really didn't understand I guessed, looked at the picture and tried to work out whether my idea worked with the rest of the story.

8 If you found a part of the story which you couldn't understand, did you continue reading the story to the end?
If so, did the meaning of the difficult bit become clear to you later on?

Yes, there was one phrase I didn't understand, but read on, then I went back to it and worked out what it meant.

9 Are you fairly confident about your reading skills in English?
   Why/why not?

Yes I have read a lot of books, some of my favourits are Clockwork Orange (Anthony Burgess), Hard Times (Charles Dickens), Crime and Punishment. I read lots of books at a time.

10 Do you enjoy reading in lessons or for pleasure or both?
   How much time do you usually spend reading?

Pleasure mostly, I read well because my mum is a teacher and taught me early to read for about 2–3 hours per day and 4–5 on holiday days.

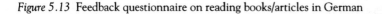

Figure 5.13 Feedback questionnaire on reading books/articles in German

work but managed to provide several lessons or parts of lessons where pupils had the opportunity to read on their own. She started the cycle by letting pupils read a book of their choice and then asking them to complete a questionnaire. The example shown in Figure 5.13 was completed by Emma.

Completing the questionnaire led on to a brainstorming session. Next lesson, the class collectively translated the Dutch poem in Chapter 4, p. 76. As she had predicted, they found the last lines of the poem difficult and she used the opportunity to model 'inferencing' and 'transfer' that had not been mentioned in the previous lesson. This and other strategies were added to the checklist. Pupils then chose another book, filling in the table like Table 4.1, p. 79, Chapter 4, which served as a reminder to use the strategies. The following week, the strategies were discussed again and pupils completed the grid once more, as they read their books. No further reminders were given and two weeks later, the pupils were asked to write down as many ways as they could of finding out the meaning of new words in a text. Finally, three weeks later, Fiona chose four pupils representing a range of attainment levels and 'personality'. They read and then summarised their chosen books for her and she observed the strategies they appeared to be using.

The pupils' responses

The questionnaires completed at the beginning of the project suggested that the high attainers more than the low attainers were already using a greater range of strategies to make sense of their chosen book, although Fiona was aware that the types of question posed may have already begun the process of teaching them new strategies. There also appeared to be a correlation between the pupils who used a wide range of strategies and their reported levels of confidence and enjoyment in reading. As the pupils were reading their books and filling in the grid, Fiona noticed the use of multiple strategies to make sense of one word; for example, 'sonnig – looks like English and there's a sun in the picture, so it must be sunny'. She also observed pupils deploying 'wild-card guessing' as discussed in Chapter 4; for example, Lee, the boy who filled in Table 4.1 shown in Chapter 4, p. 79, had not looked up the title of the book *Der Teufelstisch* (*The Devil's Table*). He assumed it meant boat and all his subsequent guesses were predicated on this initial misunderstanding: a clear demonstration of how understanding one key word can determine the level of comprehension of the text as a whole.

Using pupils' entries on their grids, Fiona drew up Table 5.3. Three high attainers had added an extra column to their grids to record a new strategy they had developed; 'splitting up words to decipher them', which is a particularly useful strategy for German.

It appeared that the high attainers translated approximately twice as many words as low attainers and used more strategies for translating each word. Their guesses are more accurate and they make greater use of cognates, the wordlist and of the pictures. From her observations in class, these high-attaining pupils seemed to pay careful attention to the details in the pictures; using the character's facial expressions, for example, and not just the objects represented. Fiona gained the impression that high attainers also made more use of grammatical clues. They knew, for example, which word was a noun and looked that up first, or which was a verb and so read the sentence aloud, logically guessing at a verb that would suit the context. (Chapter 3 noted the use of these more complex strategies in relation to Jenny's reading.) Fiona observed that:

> the more experienced, confident readers apply the simple strategies like looking for cognates, but combine these with more complex strategies such as inferencing and recognising the grammatical function of a word; thus eliminating 'wild card' guesses, which set less able learners on the wrong track.

The combination of 'top-down' and 'bottom-up' reading strategies has been discussed in earlier chapters.

Fiona acknowledged that the task asking pupils to list strategies they could remember two weeks later would not provide very reliable information, since they might either forget some that they were using or make up some that they were not using in order to please her. Nevertheless, she was disappointed to note that neither the low nor the average attainers appeared to have adopted new strategies. It seemed that high attainers remembered the highest number of strategies and used a wider range.

The 'read-aloud' interviews provided some useful insights about the role of 'personality', and not just attainment level, in pupils' use of strategies. Terry, a low attainer but one who enjoys German, made a lot of guesses, using the pictures and his knowledge of the type of story (about aliens in space). Although some guesses were incorrect, they were not illogical and did not contradict the story-line. Fiona also compared two other pupils, defined as average, noting they had very different attitudes:

Table 5.3 Pupils' use of reading strategies

Pupils	No. of words collectively listed in 25 min.	Average no. of strategies used per word	Looks like English	Guessed correctly	'Wild-card' guessing	Carried on reading	Picture helped	Asked teacher or another pupil	Used wordlist	Used dictionary	Broke up words into parts. (Added by pupils onto grid)
5 Low attainers	16	1.37	1	2	5	3	3	3	4	1	0
5 Average attainers	25	1.72	6	7	2	5	10	2	10	0	0
5 High attainers	34	1.79	11	9	1	11	9	2	15	2	3

Nick worked quickly and confidently going for overall meaning. Partly because of this, he didn't really grasp the point of the story and gave me his own précis of events at the end still unaware of any real problem! Gary was less confident and worked more using word-for-word translation . . . he often paused waiting for verbal approval. He used the wordlist more than the others and he seemed more aware of guessing wrongly.

Fiona felt that the level of motivation evident in Terry's enthusiastic reading to her, and the differences in personality between Nick and Gary were factors, over and above their attainment level, that affected their approach to tackling texts.

Future directions

Fiona felt that the cycle of strategy instruction she was able to implement over a short period of time was insufficient to have a significant impact on her class's strategy use and that low and average attainers in particular may need more extensive practice. She hopes to harness the motivation, evident in pupils such as Terry, by including more elements of choice in her lessons.

Discussion

We have followed the successes and difficulties of five different teachers working in five very different contexts as they experimented with implementing the cycle of strategy instruction; sifting through existing studies to identify appropriate strategies for their classes, translating them into accessible terms, creating space in the lessons to implement the various steps of the cycle, and finding the time to collect relevant information. We have seen some of the problems for the teachers of collecting reliable evidence, whether through questionnaires, checklists or interviews, and how hard it is to interpret it, to know what 'actually happens inside the learners' heads'. Pupils' responses to strategy instruction are open to much debate and interpretation. For example, could failure to recall strategies be due to a holiday break, or to fading out the reminders too rapidly, or to lack of opportunities for extensive practice, or simply because pupils may find it difficult to make explicit how they are learning? Marian and Jacqui's projects indicate the difficulties for practising teachers in finding the time and means to accurately assess the development of speaking skills within the constraints of the secondary school curriculum.

What conclusions can be drawn from their experiences? What are the common themes and questions that emerge in this diversity of circumstances? First, we will consider the issues raised by pupils' responses to strategy instruction before examining possible implications for the cycle.

Pupils' responses to strategy instruction

Existing use of strategies before strategy instruction

Fiona was the only teacher to administer a questionnaire before the strategy instruction in an attempt to establish what strategies the pupils were already using. Her impressions appear similar to the research findings reported in Chapter 2, that is, that successful learners use a wider range of strategies than their less successful peers, and have both the 'simple' and the more 'complex' within their repertoire.

Use of strategies after strategy instruction

THE MOST 'POPULAR' STRATEGIES

Angelina's, Pamela's and Marian's projects appear to suggest that in terms of using memorisation strategies, pupils prefer the more basic, mechanical strategies. It is difficult to establish, however, if their preferences are because they were the ones pupils were 'ready' for, in a developmental sense, or because the more complex strategies are often more time-consuming and pupils were not yet sufficiently motivated to invest the additional energy required. We will return to the issue of a possible developmental order of acquisition of strategies when we discuss the implications for teaching the cycle of learning strategies.

THE ROLE OF MOTIVATION, 'PERSONALITY' AND LEVEL OF ATTAINMENT

The issue of motivation is an important one, particularly if we consider it as part and parcel of the learner's overall 'personality', of the attitudes, level of confidence and personal learning styles that they bring to the language-learning task. Chapter 2 indicated that the correlation between level of attainment and uptake of new strategies in response to strategy instruction is far from straightforward, and the teachers here seem to have reached similar conclusions. Pupil G, a high attainer in Angelina's class, neither tried nor adopted any new strategies, whereas pupils F and L, low attainers, made considerable progress in strategy use. Similarly, pupil B in Marian's class, a proficient pupil, was more reluctant to adopt new strategies than pupil C, a less successful learner. Two average attainers in Fiona's class, Gary and Nick did not share the same approach to tackling a text. Two high attainers in Pamela's class, Kandice and Emma, responded very differently. The teachers have contrasted words like 'risk-taker', 'enthusiastic about their learning', 'confident', with 'reserved', 'serious', 'anxious'. In some cases, being anxious and careful appears to have positive effects; for example, Gary's methodical reading approach. In others, it has meant that they lacked the confidence to break with familiar patterns and embark on a new way of working. We have already seen the contrasting learning styles of Sophie, Jenny and Ben in Chapter 3. It is likely that their responses to strategy instruction would also be different. This raises the question of the extent to which strategy instruction should be directed towards capitalising on pupils' existing learning styles by making them more aware of their own personal preferred ways of learning, or should seek to alter their approach to learning. There would seem to be an argument for at least providing them with opportunities to become more self-aware and to expand their repertoire. As Rubin (1997) points out:

> If learners know only a few strategies, it is difficult for them to make choices and compare.

However, while it is one thing to encourage learners to try different strategies, it is quite another to change a 'shy', 'reserved' personality into a 'confident risk-taker'.

METACOGNITIVE AWARENESS AND ACTION PLANNING

A further related question is the differing degrees to which pupils in these class-rooms were aware of how they learned and what they needed to do to improve, or whether they needed individual guidance and support from the teacher. If we broadly refer to this as 'metacognitive awareness', it seems that some pupils like Kandice already know which strategies are most helpful for their particular problem, whereas others, as Pamela suggests, may need to understand the value of a combination of strategies to tackle their specific difficulties. It seems that the individual interviews Pamela held with some of her pupils, or the personal conversations Jacqui had with hers, helped to move forward their thinking about how to learn; to foster the 'executive control' discussed by Rubin (1992). Marian's suggestion that pupils should be encouraged to assess their own strategy development also points towards the need for each pupil to develop the capacity to reflect on and evaluate their learning. Although the action-planning stage was not built into their projects, the teachers came to recognise the assertion of O'Malley and Chamot that:

> Students without metacognitive approaches are essentially learners without direction or opportunity to review their progress, accomplishments, and future directions.
> (O'Malley *et al.* 1985: quoted in Skehan 1989, pp. 560–1)

Graham (1997, p. 123) links this heightened awareness to motivation:

> If pupils are helped to notice a link between the strategies they have employed and the resulting outcomes, their sense of control over their own learning could be enhanced and a powerful source of motivation harnessed.

It would seem then that action planning, omitted from these projects due to lack of time, is an important element of the cycle of strategy instruction.

GENDER

Making explicit what needs to be learned and how to go about it may also be of relevance in relation to gender differences in learning and attainment. The OFSTED report 'Boys and English' (HMSO 1993, p. 3) concluded that:

> Boys' performance improved when they had a clear understanding of the progress they needed to make in order to achieve well.

It is not appropriate here to examine the complex debates on boys' under-achievement. However, we have briefly alluded to some gender differences in strategy use in Chapters 2 and 3. We also note that Macaro (1997) found that boys appeared to be more receptive than girls to strategy instruction. Although boys appeared to use fewer strategies than girls before strategy instruction, when asked to comment afterwards on the effectiveness of instruction a significant proportion of them felt that it had 'made a big difference' or 'some difference'. In both cases, numbers were greater than for the girls.

Although Pamela's was a small study and the boys were not specifically asked to comment on the effectiveness of strategy instruction, their poor performance on the vocabulary tests would suggest that their response to it was less positive. Since boys are reported (Graham 1997) to find learning vocabulary particularly boring and demotivating, did the type of strategy selected (memorisation) play a part? Or was it because the nature of way the classroom was organised failed to allow them the space to meet their 'personal agenda'? The question of the balance between teacher-centred and independent learning will be discussed later in the next section, where we consider the implications of the projects for the implementation of the cycle.

Implications for the implementation of the cycle of strategy instruction

In this section we elaborate on the guiding principles for strategy instruction set out in Chapter 4 in the light of the projects described in the present chapter.

The need for extensive practice and individual dialogue between teacher and pupil

All the teachers agreed that more time was needed for the implementation of the cycle. This emerged most obviously in terms of the need for more practice and the fading out of the reminders too early. Indeed in most cases, the reminder (in the form of the checklist) was abruptly withdrawn, rather than through a series of tasks each of which made less and less explicit the links to strategies and allowed them to become automatised gradually. Rubin (1990, p. 284) points out that:

> It is increasingly clear that strategy learning requires continual and extensive training if it is to become part of a student's tool kit.

Time constraints also meant that it was difficult to achieve the kind of differentiated approach advocated by Marian, which would have allowed the teachers to ascertain for each individual pupil the most appropriate moment to withdraw the explicit teacher support. Wenden (1991, p. 107) draws on Vygotsky's notion of the 'zone of proximal development' to stress that teachers need:

> to remain in touch with the learner's changing cognitive state and so enable them to determine what kind of feedback they should provide and when training is no longer necessary.

While commenting in written form on the initial action plan is the least time-consuming form of feedback for the teachers, it would seem that a personal dialogue with some individual pupils is also important. It is easier to find time for this dialogue in an autonomous classroom than a teacher-centred one. Group work carries the additional advantage that pupils support one another through their respective 'zones of proximal development', and they can 'borrow' the understanding of their peers.

The purpose of strategy instruction should be made explicit to learners

Less obvious than the time needed for practice, but of equal importance, is the indication that more time should be devoted to explaining the rationale for strategy instruction, which was one of the guiding principles quoted in Chapter 4. We argued that this explanation was particularly important for less successful learners and the teachers have noted how some low attainers lack confidence to embark on a new approach to learning. During her interview with Joanna, Pamela appears to have used to good effect the powerful tool of persuasion suggested by Jones *et al.*:

> One of the principal goals of strategy training is to alter students' beliefs about themselves by teaching them that their failures can be attributed to the lack of effective strategies rather than to lack of ability or laziness.
>
> (Jones *et al.* 1987, p. 56)

Test results, especially where they were presented in a tangible form such as bar charts, also appear to provide a source of motivation. As Chamot and Rubin (1994, p. 773) point out:

> if strategies are presented in such a way that learners experience immediate success, they are often more willing to use them.

What emerges from the projects, however, is the need to convince not only the less successful learners but also the high attainers of the value of adopting new strategies. Jacqui and Marian indicate that, without sufficient explanation of the rationale, there is a danger that pupils remain complacent, feeling they are already achieving success and there is no need to deviate from what they are already doing. Furthermore, individual learners such as pupil B in Marian's class, who felt that some strategies simply replicated what they were already doing, clearly had not fully understood the structural value of mind-mapping, in terms of its depth of processing, rather than as the simple act of writing the words down. Indeed, the fact that pupils rejected some of the more complex strategies as being too time-consuming may indicate not simply a lack of motivation but also a lack of understanding of how memory functions. Part of the explanation of the rationale for strategy instruction might, therefore, include offering pupils insights into specific aspects of the learning process. Given that it does take time to associate a new word with another word in the mother tongue and to create a visual representation, perhaps pupils could be advised to reserve this strategy for those words whose meaning they find particularly difficult to remember. After a brainstorming session, a poster based on Table 5.4 may help. A checklist should also incorporate such guidance.

Table 5.4 Strategies for tackling problems

Your special problems	*The best strategies to try*
Can't remember particularly hard words	Associate with English word and do drawing
Can't remember gender	Associate with colours, heat/cold
Can't remember spellings	Write out words, test self
Can't say the words easily	Repeat words out loud Put words to a tune Listen to tape

Strategy instruction should involve collaborative learning

Support for this principle emerges from pupils' positive response to the opportunities Angelina, Pamela and Marian provided for them to work together. There is increasing interest (see Fawcett 1993 for example) in the value of learners carrying out 'think-alouds' together. This might be a further opportunity for pair or group activity. It would be interesting to discover, for example, what Fiona's pupils could learn from each other's approaches to reading.

Teachers of all subjects should collaborate to develop a coherent and consistent school policy in relation to strategy instruction

The teachers appear convinced that strategy instruction needs to be integrated, not only into the language-learning scheme of work, and from beginner level, but more generally into the school curriculum as a whole. They felt that otherwise opportunities were wasted for pupils to see that strategies could be transferred from one subject area to another and to provide the extensive practice so badly needed.

Further issues: strategy instruction should be geared towards the level and the needs of the learners. Which strategies? When? How?

In Chapter 4, we outlined criteria to be considered in selecting the strategies to be taught to a particular age group. These five projects would seem to indicate just how difficult it is to reach definitive conclusions about which strategies to teach when. They also illustrate the significance of the nature of the classroom organisation to be adopted. It is not possible to compare on any systematic basis the relative success or failure in the uptake of strategies across the five classrooms. At first glance, it may appear that pupils' responses to instruction in memorisation strategies yielded more positive results than in communication strategies if only because the vocabulary tests provided a tangible means of measuring progress. Yet, it would be unwise to conclude definitively that memorisation strategies are easier than communication strategies to acquire and acquired early (as the literature reviewed in Chapter 2 would seem to indicate) or easier to teach, (as argued in Chapter 4). We cannot know if Jacqui's pupils would have adopted at least some of the communication strategies, had the cycle of instruction been more systematically implemented, or if the usual format for group work had remained unchanged. Nor can we know what Angelina's pupils would have made of instruction in communication strategies. Although the pupils were older, they were low attainers and arguably may, in a developmental sense, have only been ready for straightforward memorisation strategies.

Any comparison is rendered all the more problematic, as there were different expectations from the teachers about appropriate degrees of pupil autonomy in the five classrooms. While none of the teachers adopted what Nunan (1995, p. 134) terms 'the fully autonomous end of the pedagogical continuum', there were different levels of independence offered (see Harris, in Hawkins 1996, for an illustration of steps along the continuum). It is, therefore, hard to know the extent to which the type of classroom organisation adopted by the teachers helped or hindered the acquisition of strategies. It would appear that both Angelina and Pamela found it relatively straightforward to integrate the cycle into their usual way of working with their classes; possibly because vocabulary-learning homeworks were a regular feature of most of their lessons and did not require additional time. Although both of them provided opportunities for pair and group practice and discussion, the organisation of the classroom remained largely teacher-centred. In Fiona's case, it was more difficult to integrate strategy instruction into her usual lessons, as she had to find time to incorporate not only the teaching of reading strategies but also opportunities for pupils to read on their own. The organisation of Marian's and Jacqui's classroom was different in that pupils spent the majority of their lessons working in groups, although the desire to foster speaking skills was not the sole reason for this. Both teachers sought to be realistic by not asking pupils to take full responsibility for what was to be learned and how. However, more discussion as to how the pupils chose which task to undertake, and what doing it told them about their strengths and weaknesses might have been more beneficial in developing the pupils' meta-cognitive strategies and their sense of responsibility than simply asking them if they enjoyed the task. Does presenting pupils with a list of tasks to be completed, where the only choice they have is the pace at which they work and the order in which to undertake the tasks provide an initial, gentle step along the road to autonomy, or simply become another classroom routine to be accomplished mechanically? Given that Jacqui's experiences seem to underline the importance of 'one thing at a time', of not 'overwhelming' pupils with too many new things to cope with at once, where does the teacher, who wants to shift control from herself to the learners, start? We have acknowledged the dangers of 'tacking on' strategy instruction to an otherwise traditional form of teaching and the value of collaborative learning. We see the relationship between strategic competence, communicative competence and autonomy as one of interdependence, each feeding into the other. Figure 5.14 offers a representation.

We recall the conclusion of Little (1997) that:

> If the pursuit of autonomy requires that we focus explicitly on the strategic component of language learning and language use, the reverse should also be the case: focus on strategies should lead us to learner autonomy.

How are these dual goals to be pursued in practice? One possibility would be a spiral model, where more autonomous ways of working are gradually introduced, interspersed with instruction in strategies that themselves become ever more complex and match the new opportunities that pupils are being offered.

In this, it is important to avoid the danger that such a model, at least at the beginner stage, might be reduced to a series of lessons where pupils are intro-duced to sets of strategies, with only limited opportunities to deploy them. Opportunities for the development of metacognitive strategies could be delayed,

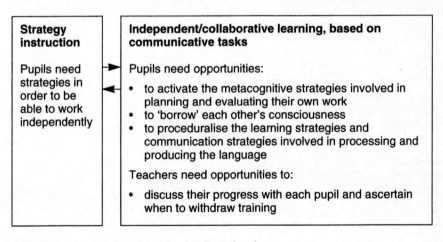

Figure 5.14 Strategy instruction and independent learning

and yet it is these which appear to be significant both in enabling pupils to make responsible decisions in what to learn, rather than performing tasks mindlessly, and about how to learn so that pupils are able themselves to activate the appropriate strategies. This returns us to the issue of progression that was discussed in earlier chapters. These projects have served to highlight the need for a full understanding of possible developmental orders through which strategies can be acquired and for reliable evidence of the types of classroom organisation that are most likely to foster strategy acquisition.

Conclusion

In this chapter we have looked in some detail at a group of teachers attempting to develop learning strategies with their pupils. The examples we quote show up the messiness of real-life teaching when compared to methodological intention. Nevertheless, we would argue that even over the course of the limited period of time available, what the teachers had to report strengthens rather than weakens the case for giving strategies a higher profile in the modern-languages classroom. We have drawn out some of the issues and principles which may guide others looking to work on strategies with their pupils. We want to draw our discussion to a close in the concluding chapter of the book by again thinking about the whole domain of learning strategies and what they imply for the theory and practice of modern-language teaching. We also wish to consider further what this means for the teacher and their traditional teaching role.

Conclusion

We started out in the introduction by asking: why a book about learning strategies? In the course of five chapters we have attempted to demonstrate some of the rationale for and uses of learning strategies. In Part One we set out the historical context of methodological reform and the types of learning theories and approaches which have governed classroom teaching in modern languages. In Part Two we offered some practical examples of learning strategies in use, and discussed what happened when a group of teachers attempted to 'instruct' their pupils in strategy usage. In the original title of our book – *Learning to Learn* – we intended to point towards a different emphasis in the learning of a second language; from teacher input to pupil autonomy. In language-learning terms, the past century can be seen as a search for methodological perfection: in other words, a view that if we can polish methodological procedure, then we can maximise the effectiveness of teaching and the efficiency of learning. However, to echo the words of Palmer quoted earlier: it has not so much been methodology we lack, as the underlying bases of understanding which can justify classroom methods. In terms of learning theory, we have seen stages of development in our understanding of just what language is, how it operates, and the processes of acquiring it. Who is to say whether or not (how, and to what extent) recent past orthodoxies in language-learning theories – the monitor model, Chomskyan linguistics, cognitive theory – will be superseded, modified, or fall into disrepute, in the same way as behaviourist linguistics are today considered to be outmoded? Such is the nature of any developing field of knowledge.

If we think for a moment about the successes of modern-languages teaching, then we can see that people have indeed learned foreign languages one way or another; that there are thousands of individuals walking around who are competent to understand and be understood in one, two, three or more foreign languages. Unless they have been plunged into a bilingual environment where they have to sink or swim, this success has been achieved with the aid of modern-language teaching, including whatever methodological imperfections this may now be seen to involve. We also know that only a minority of second-language teachers subscribe to a single methodology. Most draw on a range of techniques, approaches, and personal understandings adapted for the particular learning context and the needs, both explicit and implicit, of the learners with whom they are faced.

However, if we view modern-language teaching in a more critical light, we can see that the ambitious aims and objectives of policy and practice have not always delivered the goods: materials do not always do what their authors claim they will; pupils do not progress as anticipated; take-up in advanced language courses remains static. The past twenty years or so have seen a revolution in modern-language teaching in Britain, and the communicative movement has swept along almost everything and everyone in its path. On one level, there never has been greater opportunity for creating lively, attractive, interactive modern-language lessons, for maximising target-language use, and making the culture of the language 'come alive' for pupils. We know from national surveys that pupils' attitudes and interest in foreign languages is often extremely positive and enthusiastic, especially in the early years of language learning. However, we also know that progress often slows down or peters out at an intermediate level, and many pupils remain unable to initiate and develop linguistic exchanges for their own purposes. Teachers too have grown wary of the 'hype' surrounding use of the target language as an end in itself. Faced with methodological disappointments, many turn back to grammar as providing a method that works.

Our discussion in this book has faced the reality of this situation. We would not want to prescribe yet another alternative methodology or a panacea for perceived underachievement of learners in modern languages. Instead, we recognise that it is a multifaceted problem. Good language learning does begin with the pupil and the activities with which they are involved. Yet, classroom practice is often mostly determined by the teacher. Good language learning does therefore involve some description of good teaching. The message of this book is that such good modern-language learning and teaching might best be facilitated by a reorientation of practice in the languages classroom, but this reorientation needs to originate in shifts in understanding of the processes of language learning and consequent teaching, rather than a new methodological trend. Our consideration of the possible direction of this shift has focused around the notion of autonomy and around a cycle of strategy instruction designed to facilitate it.

As we enter the new millennium, the state of education in many countries is rife with conflicting elements and internal forces. For much of our century, the teaching of any school subject in school was often regarded as instruction through explanation and rote memorisation. Then, in the 1960s, and with greater social awareness and focus on individual liberties, this traditional approach to learning and teaching gave way to a more open style. 'Pupil-centred learning' became a byword for good practice and the accent was more on individual pupil expression than achievement measured against a notional gold standard. For most of the 1980s in Britain, and half of the 1990s, an enormous process of social and economic reform took place as a result of the policy of the government of the day. Its aims were, supposedly, to free people from the confines of state control, tax and interference in their lives. Paradoxically, however, this socio-economic 'liberalisation' was limited to the financial and management structures as far as schools were concerned; while what was taught and how became increasingly under central state control. Progressive education became a pejorative term and there was a sense of need to get back to basics in the classroom. Nowhere was this more evident than in the controversy in teaching literacy where pupil-centred 'real books' were criticised for not being rigorous enough in developing the necessary reading skills of young children. The more instructional 'phonics' were prescribed as medicine for below-international averages in the reading abilities of the nation's children.

This movement continues seemingly unabated. The concern with literacy has spawned a 'literacy hour' in our schools with its set content of activities for teachers to follow. There is also a national numeracy project which sets out to improve the mathematical skills of children in a nation now apparently addicted to the calculator and computer. Teachers do not do as they judge best but as they are instructed by centrally produced documentation.

Autonomy might then be considered to be furthest from the minds of educators and policy makers. Yet, to accept this view would be an oversimplification of a complex age. The liberalisation of the 1980s and 1990s continues. There is a strong thrust in emphasising individual responsibility. National and European citizenship is expressed in terms of what the individual can do for the community as much as it can do for them. In teaching and learning, also, individual learner profiles and targets very much form part of the new approaches to classroom practice. For example, the national literacy strategy itself contains the kind of skills individual pupils need to help them in their learning: reading textbooks, collecting information, etc. Certainly, it is recognised that true progress in learning involves some sort of 'making-it-your-own'. Garrigan (1997) claims that learner autonomy exists when learners are aware of themselves; when they know and understand the learning context; have the skills necessary to function in this context and set their own learning agenda. His own preoccupation is with why advanced-level students should achieve this sort of autonomy and how they might be best assisted. Autonomy, in this sense, is defined not in terms of some notional idealism of individual expression but as a necessary stage in the true learning of any subject. Clearly, a competent individual in whatever subject is autonomous in that they can act independently within a given context.

It is also recognised that autonomy of this type does not arise *ex nihilo* out of nowhere; it is not something that is won as a final, ultimate step in the stages of progression through which an individual passes. Rather, such autonomy is fostered slowly, bit by bit at every point on the path of learning. Strategies for learning (Coles and White 1997), active approaches to learning (Coles and White 1993), TASC (thinking actively in a social context) (Wallace and Adams 1993), thinking skills (Blagg *et al.* 1988), thinking tactics (Lake and Needham n.d.), accelerated learning: these are the type of conceptual skills now being developed with pupils at every stage of their learning and in a range of subject areas. Our cycle of learning-strategy instruction is a close relative of these more general approaches to learning.

The message in this book offers a way and a reason for adopting a similar strategic approach to modern-language learning and teaching. It is linked to autonomy in that we recognise that in order to be linguistically competent, an individual needs to have independent language skills. Moreover, in order to achieve this independence, they each need the means to get there. As Dam (1990) points out: ' The aim is learner autonomy – learner autonomy is the only means possible' (p. 20). For the teacher, this is likely to involve a greater sensitivity to individual learning styles and the learning strategies they necessarily entail than has often hitherto been the case – even in the communicative classroom. It therefore must involve offering learners choices about what and how to learn. We believe such an emphasis is justifiable not only for principled, pedagogic reasons but in terms of what we now know about the processes of language learning *per se*. Clearly, the models of the past paid insufficient attention to the fluid, shifting nature of language as it arises in and between individuals and in a myriad of contexts. Some of these earlier models captured something of the nature of language, but the cognitive approach outlined in this book expresses more of the reality of competence as something that is in a continual state of flux in the current of learning contexts, only some of which would be pedagogic. However, although this theoretical perspective is dynamic, it is no less rigorous for that. We believe that the whole approach to autonomy now advocated in education circles and the strategies to be employed to bring this about, examples of which in terms of modern languages can be found in this book, only make sense if understood through an underlying theoretical rationale. If the theory and practice of learning strategies in modern-languages learning and teaching do not go hand in hand, then they will be mishandled in the classroom, or used as a cure-all, or as yet another entertaining gimmick, which have in the past promised more than they have delivered. Theory is not popular these days in many spheres of education. Educational research and theory is often seen as out of touch, or irrelevant to classroom practice; as not connecting with teachers' ways and needs. This is not an issue we can unpick in the present context (for a more developed treatment, see Grenfell 1997). We do however raise the relationship between theory and practice and how this has implications which vary for the researcher, the teacher, and the pupils. We want to encourage an approach to modern-languages teaching that is principled; that is based on both theoretical thinking and practical explorations. In neither case, though, can this be done exclusively by professional outsiders to the daily practice of classroom teaching. It must come from the teachers and the pupils themselves. Otherwise, it is a contradiction in terms. How can teachers develop autonomy in their pupils if they themselves have no say in whether and how it is to be implemented? The whole point of autonomy and strategy work is that this degree of individual self-definition in language learning and teaching should come from those involved most directly with it. However, and this is a crucial issue to which we have returned at different points in this book, such autonomy and strategy work never advocates total withdrawal from, or abandonment of all other methods, or a rejection of the teacher. Independence should not be considered synonymous with isolation. Nevertheless, it does imply a less restricted, and prescribed syllabus or curriculum than is presently the case. To bring a cliché to mind, it sometimes seems as if pupils are being taught to pass a certain exam at a certain level rather than to learn a modern-foreign language. The National Curriculum in Modern Foreign Languages in England has none of the prescribed content of past syllabuses. However, it does set out a very definite programme for teaching. Progression is defined according to particular chosen elements, while others are left out. Developing competence is understood to take place incrementally and to be mostly dependent on observable linguistic products. Clearly, much of what we have presented in this book suggests a rather more complex and sophisticated view of the processes of developing linguistic competence. And yet every teacher of modern foreign languages in the land has to teach according to the framework, and, incidentally, is inspected (and thus publicly accountable) according to how successfully they are deemed to deliver it. Autonomy in language learning for pupils must imply a degree of autonomy for teachers in how to teach. The crucial issue is how best to encourage a thinking profession, to produce teachers who are methodologically inquisitive enough to develop classroom practice. Teachers need the space and the time to improve practice, while remaining accountable for how lessons are conducted and what they ultimately result in for the pupils in terms of enhanced linguistic competence. Such a situation cannot be brought about by telling teachers what to do, in the same way that telling pupils how to learn does not necessarily bring about language learning automatically.

The final issue we would therefore wish to raise in conclusion to this book is that of teacher training and continuing professional development. We know from research carried out into teacher education and from more anecdotal evidence that teachers are often resentful of others telling them what to do in the classroom, whether they be government employees or researchers into language teaching and learning. Advocating a strategic approach for pupils might then be seen as just another prescription; as something else to do in the classroom. This initial barrier has to be overcome. In our own case examples, we have seen teachers taking learning strategies on board as a result of their own dissatisfaction with the methods and techniques they are employing. Getting teachers to use strategy instruction with their pupils therefore starts with their own needs and then leads into an investigation of the underlying theory for such practice. Very often, teachers need to experience directly the use of strategies themselves, for example by doing exercises like the Dutch poem earlier quoted, rather than being simply told of their value. Most effective implementation of strategy work with pupils occurs where teachers work in collaboration; both with modern foreign languages colleagues and those from other subject areas. Finally, as in any training, trainers themselves must know when to provide structured support and when to gradually withdraw. Indeed, many of the principles for training teachers in strategy instruction are not dissimilar to those for language learning. In both cases, those involved have not only to do what they are told but think about what to do and why, to make choices and decisions, and commit themselves to their own aims and objectives. This is the sense of learning to learn rather than simply being taught. The latter can too often be passive and be too focused on the 'other'. What we have sought to suggest throughout this book is that teaching alone is not an effective or efficient way of proceeding methodologically. A more holistic approach is needed rather than a latest methodological fashion. Working around the notion of autonomy; developing learning strategies for pupils; creating space for teachers' professional thinking and development; enquiring in a more principled way into the processes of language itself will help to bring this learning to learn into being as we cross into the twenty-first century.

References

Anderson, J. R. (1983) *The Architecture of Cognition*, Cambridge, MA: Harvard University Press.

Anderson, J. R. (1985) *Cognitive Psychology and its Implications*, 2nd edn, New York: Freeman.

Anthony, E. M. (1963) 'Approach, method and technique', *English Language Teaching*, 17: 63–7.

Austin, J. L. (1962) *How to do Things with Words*, London: Oxford University Press.

Bachman, L. F. (1990) *Fundamental Considerations in Language Testing*, Oxford: Oxford University Press.

Bacon, S. M. (1992) 'The relationship between gender, comprehension, processing strategies, and cognitive and affective response in foreign language listening', *The Modern Language Journal*, 76(ii): 160–76.

Bialystok, E. (1984) 'Strategies in interlanguage and performance', in Davies, A., Croper C. and Howatt, A. P. R. (eds) *Interlanguage*, Edinburgh: Edinburgh University Press.

Bialystok, E. (1990) *Communication Strategies: A Psychological Analysis of Second Language Use*, Oxford: Blackwell.

Blagg, N., Ballinger, M., Gardner, R. and Petty, M. (1988) *Somerset Thinking Skills Course: Modules 1–7*, Oxford: Blackwell.

Bourdieu, P. (1991) *Language and Symbolic Power*, Cambridge: Polity Press.

Bourrhis, R.Y. (1982) 'Language policies and language attitudes: le monde de la francophonie', in Ryan, E.B. and Giles, H. (eds) *Attitudes Towards Language Variation: Social and Applied Contexts*, London: Edward Arnold.

Broady, E. and Kenning, M. (1996) *Promoting Learner Autonomy in University Language Teaching*, London: CILT.

Brumfit, C. J. (1984) *Communicative Methodology in Language Teaching*, Cambridge: Cambridge University Press.

Brumfit, C. J. (1988) 'Applied linguistics and communicative language teaching', *Annual Review of Applied Linguistics* 8: 3–13.

Bügel, K. and Buunk, B. P. (1996) 'Sex differences in foreign language text comprehension: the role of interests and prior knowledge', *The Modern Language Journal*, 80(i): 15–29.

Canale, M. (1983) 'From communicative competence to communicative language pedagogy', in Richards, J. C. and Schmidt, R. W. (eds) *Language and Communication*, London: Longman.

Canale, M. and Swain, M. (1980) 'Theoretical bases of communicative approaches to second language teaching and testing', *Applied Linguistics* 1(1) 1–47.

Carr, W. and Kemmis, S. (1986) *Becoming Critical: Education, Knowledge and Action Research*, London: Falmer Press.

Carrell, P. L., Pharis, B. G. and Liberto, J. C. (1989) 'Metacognitive strategy training for ESL reading', *TESOL Quarterly* 23(4): 647–78.

Chamot, A. U. and Rubin, J. (1994) 'Comments on Janie Rees-Miller's "A critical appraisal of learner training: theoretical bases and teaching implications. Two readers react', *TESOL Quarterly Forum* 28(4): 771–6.

Chesterfield, R. and Chesterfield, K. B. (1985) 'Natural order in children's use of second language learning strategies', *Applied Linguistics*, 6(1): 45–59.

Chomsky, N. (1957) *Syntactic Structures*, The Hague: Mouton.

Chomsky, N. (1965) *Aspects of the Theory of Syntax*, Cambridge, MA: MIT Press.

CILT (1989) *Information Sheet No. 12*, London: CILT.

Clark, A. and Trafford, J. (1996) 'Return to gender: boys' and girls' attitudes and achievements', *Language Learning Journal*, 14: 40–9.

Clark, J. (1987) *Curriculum Renewal in School Foreign Language Learning*, Oxford: Oxford University Press.

Coles, M. and White, C. (1993) *Learning Matters: Active Approaches to Studying*, Carlisle: CAREL Press.

Coles, M. and White, C. (1997) *Strategies for Studying*, Carlisle: CAREL Press.

Council for Cultural Co-operation Education Committee (1996) *Modern Languages: Learning, Teaching and Assessment. A Common European Framework of Reference*, Strasbourg: Council of Europe.

Dam, L. (1990) *Learner Autonomy 3: From Theory to Classroom Practice*, Dublin: Authentik Language Learning Resources Ltd.

Department for Education (1993) *Boys and English*, Report from the Office of Her Majesty's Chief Inspector for Schools, London: HMSO.

Department of Education and Science (1985) *The National Criteria for GCSE*, London: HMSO.

Department of Education and Science (1990) *National Curriculum: Modern Foreign Languages Working Group Initial Advice*, London: HMSO.

Department for Education (1995) *Modern Foreign Languages in the National Curriculum*, London: HMSO.

Dickinson, L. (1987) *Self-instruction in Language Learning*, Cambridge: Cambridge University Press.

Dickinson, L. (1995) 'Autonomy and motivation: a literature review', *System*, 23(2): 165–74.

Donato, R. and McCormick, D. (1994) 'A sociocultural perspective on language learning strategies: the role of mediation', *The Modern Language Journal*, 78(iv): 453–64.

Edmunds, M. (1995) 'Problem-solving using classroom research: some experiments in improving writing, motivation and learning' in *Modern Languages Policy and Practice*, 1, Stirling: Scottish CILT.

Ellis, R. (1990) *Instructed Second Language Acquisition*, Oxford: Blackwell.

Faerch, C. and Kasper, G. (eds) (1987) *Introspection in Second Language Research*, Clevedon: Multilingual Matters.

Fawcett, G. (1993) 'Using students as think aloud models', *Reading Research and Instruction*, 33(2): 95–104.

Garfinkel, H. (1968) *Studies in Ethnomethodology*, London: Polity Press.

Garrigan, P. (1997) 'Some key factors in the promotion of learner autonomy in higher education', *Journal of Further and Higher Education*, 21(2): 169–82.

Gathercole, I (ed.) (1990) *Autonomy in Language Learning*, London: CILT.

Giles, H. (ed.) (1977) *Language, Ethnicity and Intergroup Relations*, London: Academic Press.

Gillette, B. (1994) 'The role of learner goals in L2 success', in Lantolf, J. P. and Appel, G. (eds) *Vygotskyian Approaches to Second Language Research*.

Graham, S. (1997) *Effective Language Learning*, Clevedon: Multilingual Matters.

Graham, S. and Rees, F. (1995) 'Gender differences in language learning: the question of control', *Language Learning Journal*, 11: 18–19.

Grenfell, M. (1997) 'Theory and practice in modern language teacher training', *Language Learning Journal*, 16: 28–34.

Grenfell, M. (1998a) 'Theory, practice and pedagogic research' in Grenfell, M. and James, D. *Bourdieu and Education: Acts of Practical Theory*, London: Falmer Press.

Grenfell, M. (1998b) *Training Teachers in Practice*, Clevedon: Multilingual Matters.

Grenfell, M. and Harris, V. (1993) 'How do pupils learn? Part 1', *Language Learning Journal*, 8: 22–5.

Grenfell, M. and Harris, V. (1994) 'How do pupils learn? Part 2', *Language Learning Journal*, 9, 7–11.

Grenfell, M. and Harris, V. (1995) 'Learning strategies and the advanced language learner'. Paper given at the conference of the *British Association of Applied Linguistics*, Southampton.

Grice, H. (1975) 'Logic and Conversation', in Cole, P. and Morgan, J. (eds) *Syntax and Semantics: Speech Acts*, New York: Academic Press.

Halliday, M. A. K. (1978) *Language as Social Semiotic. The Social Interpretation of Language and Meaning*, London: Arnold.

Harding, A., Page, B. and Rowell, S., (1980) *Graded Objectives in Modern Languages*, London: CILT.

Harris, V. (1996) 'Developing pupil autonomy', in Hawkins, E. (ed.) *30 Years of Language Teaching*, London: CILT.

Harris, V. (1997) *Teaching Learners How To Learn; Strategy Training in the ML Classroom*, London: CILT.

Hawkins, E. (1987) *Modern Languages in the Curriculum*, rev. edn, Cambridge: Cambridge University Press.

Holec, H. (ed.) (1988) *Autonomy and Self-directed Learning: Present Fields of Application*, Strasbourg: Council of Europe.

Holec, H. (1996) 'Self-directed learning: an alternative form of training', in Holec, H., Little, D. and Richterich, R. *Strategies in Language Learning and Use*, Strasbourg: Council of Europe.

Hopkins, D. (1993) *A Teacher's Guide to Classroom Research*, Milton Keynes: Open University Press.

Hosenfeld, C., Arnold, V., Kirchofer, J., Laciura, J. and Wilson, L. (1981) 'Second language reading: a curricular sequence for teaching reading strategies', *Foreign Language Annals*, 14(5): 415–22.

Howatt, A. P. R. (1984) *A History of English Language Teaching*, Oxford: Oxford University Press.

Hymes, D. ([1967] 1972) 'On communicative competence', in Pride, J. B. and Holmes J. (eds) *Sociolinguistics*, Harmondsworth: Penguin.

Johnstone, R. (1989) *Communicative Interaction: A Guide for Language Teachers*, London: CILT.

Jones, B. F., Palinscar, A. S., Ogle, D. S. and Carr, E. G. (1987) *Strategic Teaching and*

Learning: Cognitive Instruction in the Content Area, Alexandria, VA: Association for Supervision and Curriculum Development.

Kellerman, E. (1991) 'Compensatory strategies in second language research: a critique, a revision, and some (non) implications for the classroom', in Phillipson, R., Kellerman, E., Selinker, L., Sharwood-Smith, M. and Swain M. (eds) *Foreign/Second Language Pedagogy Research*, Clevedon: Multilingual Matters.

Kern, R. G. (1989) 'Second Language reading strategy instruction: its effects on comprehension and word inference ability', *Modern Language Journal* 73(2): 135–49.

Krashen, S. (1981) *Second Language Acquisition and Second Language Learning*, Oxford: Pergamon Press.

Krashen, S. (1982) *Principles and Practice in Second Language Acquisition*, Oxford: Pergamon Press

Krashen, S. and Seliger, L. (1976) 'The role of formal and informal linguistic environments in adult second language acquisition', *International Journal of Applied Linguistics*, 3: 15–21.

Labov, W. (1972) *Sociolinguistic Patterns*, Philadelphia, PA: University of Pennsylvania Press.

Lake, M. and Needham, M. (n.d.) *Top Ten Tactics*, Birmingham: Questions Publishing.

Lantolf, J. and Frawley, W. (1983) 'Second language performance and Vygotskyian psycholinguistics', LACUS Forum.

Lantolf J. and Appel, G. (eds) *Vygotskian Approaches to Second Language Learning*, New Jersey: Ablex.

Little, D. (ed.) (1989) *Self-Access Systems for Language Learning*. Dublin: Authentik, CILT.

Little, D. (1994) *Strategies in Language Learning and Teaching: some Introductory Reflections*, Mimeo, Trinity College, Dublin.

Little, D. (1996) 'Strategic competence considered in relation to strategic control of the language learning process', in Holec, H., Little D. and Richterich, R. *Strategies in Language Learning and Use*, Strasbourg: Council of Europe.

Little, D. (1997) 'Strategies in language learning and teaching: some introductory reflections'. Paper given at the CILT Research Forum 'Strategies in Language Learning', 22 February.

Little, D., Devitt, S. and Singleton, D. (1989) *Learning Foreign Languages from Authentic Texts: Theory and Practice*, Dublin: Authentik Language Learning Resources Ltd.

Littlewood, W. (1981) *Communicative Language Teaching*, Cambridge: Cambridge University Press.

Longman Concise English Dictionary (1985), Harlow: Longman.

Loulidi, R. (1990) 'Is language learning really a female business?', *Language Learning Journal*, Spring, 40–3.

Low, L., Duffield, J., Brown, S. and Johnstone, R. (1993) *Evaluating Foreign Languages in Primary Schools*, Stirling: Scottish CILT.

Macaro, E. (1997) 'Gender differences in strategy use'. Paper given at the CILT Research Forum 'Strategies in Language Learning', 22 February.

McDonough, S. H. (1995) *Strategy and Skill in Learning a Foreign Language*, London: Edward Arnold.

McLaughlin, B. (1978) 'The monitor model: some methodological considerations', *Language Learning*, 28: 309–32.

Mitchell, R. (1997) *Progression in Foreign Language Learning*, Centre for Language in Education Occasional Paper No. 45: University of Southampton.

Naiman, N., Fröhlich, M., Stern, H. H. and Todesco, A. (1978/1996) *The Good Language Learner*, Clevedon: Multilingual Matters.

Nunan, D. (1995) 'Closing the gap between learning and instruction', *TESOL Quarterly* 29(1): 133–58.

OFSTED (1995) *Modern Foreign languages; A Review of Inspection Findings, 1993/4*, London: HMSO.

O'Malley (1987) 'The effects of training in the use of learning strategies on acquiring English as a second language', in Wenden, A. L. and Rubin, J. (eds) *Learner Strategies in Language Learning*, Hemel Hampstead: Prentice Hall International English Language Teaching.

O'Malley, J. M., and Chamot, A. U. (1988) 'How to teach learning strategies', in Chamot, A. U., O'Malley, J. M. and Küpper, L. (eds) *The Cognitive Academic Language Learning Approach (CALLA) Training Manual*, Arlington, VA: Second Language Learning.

O'Malley, J. M. and Chamot, A. U. (1990) *Language Learning Strategies in Second Language Acquisition*, Cambridge: Cambridge University Press.

O'Malley, J. M., Chamot, A. U., Stewner-Manzanares, G., Kupper, L. and Russo, R. P. (1985) 'Learning strategy applications with students of English as a second language', *TESOL Quarterly*, 19: 285–96.

Oxford, R. (1990) *Language Learning Strategies: What Every Teacher Should Know*, Boston: Heinle and Heinle.

Oxford, R. (1993) 'Research on second language learning strategies', *Annual Review of Applied Linguistics*, 13: 175–87.

Page, B. (ed.) (1992) *Letting Go–Taking Hold*, London: CILT.

Palmer, H. E. (1917) *The Scientific Study and Teaching of Languages*, London: Harrap. (Revised, Harper, D. (ed.), Oxford: Oxford University Press, 1968.)

Parry, K. (1993) 'The social construction of reading strategies: new directions for research', *Journal for Research in Reading*, 16(2): 148–56.

Piaget, J. (1926) *The Language and Thought of the Child*, New York: Harcourt Brace.

Politzer, R. L. (1983) 'An exploratory study of self-reported language learning behaviors and their relation to achievement', *Studies in Second Language Acquisition*, 6: 54–68.

Rendall, H. (1998) *Stimulating Grammatical Awareness: A Fresh Look at Language Acquisition*, London: CILT.

Reynolds, R. (1995) 'Boys and English. So what's the problem?', *The English and Media Magazine*, 33: 15–18.

Rivers, W. and Temperley, M. (1978) *A Practical Guide to the Teaching of English*, Oxford: Oxford University Press.

Rubin, J. (1975) 'What the "good language learner" can teach us', *TESOL Quarterly* 9: 41–51.

Rubin, J. (1981) 'Study of cognitive processes in second language learning', *Applied Linguistics*, 11 117–31.

Rubin, J. (1990) 'How learner strategies can inform language teaching', in Bickley, V. (ed.) *Language Use, Language Teaching and the Curriculum*, Institute of Language in Education: Hong Kong.

Rubin, J. (1992) 'Helping language learners develop executive control'. Paper presented at the LEND conference on Learner Autonomy, Montecatini, Italy. 31 October.

Rubin, J. (1997) 'Developing, monitoring and evaluating'. Paper presented at AAAL conference, 11 March.

Saussure, F. de ([1916] 1974) *Course in General Linguistics*, tr. Baskin, W. Glasgow: Collins.

Schön, D. (1983) *The Reflective Practitioner: How Professionals Think in Action*, London: Temple Smith.

Schön, D. (1987) *Educating the Reflective Practitioner: Toward a New Design for Teaching and Learning in the Professions*, San Francisco: Jossey Bass.

Searle, J. R. (1969) *Speech Acts*, Cambridge: Cambridge University Press.

Seliger, H. W. (1983) 'The language learner as linguist: of metaphors and realities', *Applied Linguistics*, 4: 179–91.

Sheerin, S. (1989) *Self-Access*, Oxford: Oxford University Press.

Shiffrin, R. M. and Schneider, W. (1977) 'Controlled and automatic information processing: perceptual learning, automatic attending and a general theory', *Psychological Review*, 84: 127–90.

Skehan, P. (1989) *Individual Differences in Second Language Learning*, London: Edward Arnold.

Skehan, P. and Foster, P. (1997) 'Task type and task processing conditions as influences on foreign language performance', *Language Teaching Research*, 1(3): 185–211.

Spender, D. (1980) *Man Made Language*, London: Routledge & Kegan Paul.

Stern, H. H. (1975) 'What can we learn from the Good Language Learner?', *Canadian Modern Language Review*, 31: 304–18.

Swarbrick, A. (1990) *Reading for Pleasure in a Foreign Language*, London: CILT.

Tajfel, H. (1982) 'The social psychology of minorities', in Husband, C. (ed.) *Race in Britain: Continuity and Change*, Hutchinson UL.

Taylor, T. J. (1992) *Mutual Misunderstanding: Scepticism and the Theorising of Language and Interpretation*, London: Routledge.

Thompson, I. and Rubin, J. (1996) 'Can strategy instruction improve listening comprehension?', *Foreign Language Annals*, 29(3): 331–42.

Van Ek, J. (1975) *The Threshold Level*, Strasbourg: Council of Europe.

Vygotsky, L. S. (1962) *Thought and Language*, Cambridge, MA: MIT Press.

Vygotsky, L. S. (1978) *Mind in Society*. Cambridge, MA: Harvard University Press.

Wallace, B. and Adams, H. (1993) *TASC: Thinking Actively in a Social Context*, Bicester: AB Academic Publishers.

Weinstein, C. E. and Underwood, V. L. (1985) 'Learning strategies: the how of learning', in Segal, J., Chipman S. and Glaser R. (eds) *Relating Instruction to Research*, Hillsdale, NJ: Erlbaum.

Wenden, A. L. (1986) 'Helping L2 learners think about learning', *English Language Teaching Journal* 40: 3–12.

Wenden, A. L. (1987) 'Incorporating learner training in the classroom', in Wenden A. L. and Rubin J. (eds) *Learner Strategies in Language Learning*, Hemel Hampstead: Prentice Hall International English Language Teaching.

Wenden, A. L. (1991) *Learner Strategies for Learner Autonomy*, Hemel Hempstead: Prentice Hall.

Wenden, A. and Rubin, J. (1987) *Learning Strategies in Language Learning*, Englewood Cliffs, NJ: Prentice Hall.

Wesche, M. B. (1981) 'Language aptitude measures in streaming, matching students with methods, and diagnosis of learning problems', in Diller K. C. (ed.) *Individual Differences and Universals in Language Learning Aptitude*, Rowley MA: Newbury House.

Widdowson, H. G. (1978) *Teaching Language as Communication*, Oxford: Oxford University Press.

Wilkins, D. A. (1976) *Notional Syllabuses*, Oxford: OUP.

Witkin, H. A. (1962) *Psychological Differentiation*, Wiley: New York.

Witkin, H. A., Goodennough, D. and Oltman, P. (1979) 'Psychological differentiation: current status', *Journal of Personality and Social Psychology*, 37: 1127–45.

Wong Fillmore (1979) 'Individual differences in second language acquisition', in Fillimore, C. J., Wang, W. S. Y. and Kempler, D. (eds) *Individual Differences in Language Ability and Behaviour*, New York: Academic Press.

Index

accuracy 55
action planning 104–5, 140; checking
    written work 95; communication
    strategies 101, 103; for listening skills
    82, 84–5, 87; for memorisation skills
    87, 88, 93; reading strategies 77–80
active strategy 37, 38
Adams, A. 87, 92
Adams, H. 149
adaptive control of thinking (ACT)
    model 44
age 48; see also level of learners
all-purpose words 62
Anderson, J.R. 44
Anglund, J.W. 108
Anthony, E.M. 10
anthropology 18
applied language studies 1, 8
approach: method, technique and 10–11,
    19–20
attainment, level of 135–8, 139–40
attribution theory 73
audio-lingual methods 12–13
audio-visual methods 12–13
auditory monitoring 89, 94
authenticity of language 21
autonomy, learner's 34–6, 39–40, 50, 104,
    148–50; teachers' projects on strategy
    instruction and 111–13, 117–18,
    118–20, 144–6
autonomy, teacher's 50, 150–1
avoidance strategies 62
awareness raising 75, 83, 88, 94, 99, 102

Bachman, L.F. 17
beginner learners 63–6, 74–5, 106;
    teaching learning strategies to 75–87
behaviourism 12–14
Bialystok, E. 39

Blagg, N. 149
Bourdieu, P. 8
boys: underachievement 111, 141; see also
    gender differences
Brumfit, C.J. 17–18, 19

Canale, M. 16–17
Centre for Information on Language
    Teaching and Research (CILT) 20
Chamot, A.U. 38, 46, 62, 74, 75, 89, 127;
    metacognitive strategies 45, 104, 120,
    140
checking written work 87–91; strategy
    instruction 94–7
Chesterfield, K.B. 46, 69
Chesterfield, R. 46, 69
Chomsky, N. 14–16
Chomskyan linguistics 14–19
circumlocution 93, 99, 100
Clark, A. 66
Clark, J. 22
classical humanism 22
cognitive strategies 44–6
cognitive style 46–8, 67–8
cognitive theory 42–6
Coles, M. 149
collaborative learning 105, 117–18,
    123–5, 143
Common European Framework 49–50,
    104
common sense, modelling using 83
communication strategies 37, 38, 39, 58,
    62–3, 91–8; strategy instruction
    99–103; teacher's project 127–32
communicative competence 16–17, 31,
    49
communicative language teaching
    (CLT) 1, 2, 14–28; Chomskyan
    linguistics 14–19; curriculum reform

White, C. 149
Wilkins, D.A. 22
Witkin, H.A. 47
Wong Fillmore 39, 129
Wright, F. 109
writing down sounds 84

written word 7, 59, 61–2; teaching
    strategies for checking written work
    87–91, 94–5, 96, 97
written work *see* checking

zone of proximal development 142